PANIC RULES!

Everything You Need to Know About the Global Economy

By Robin Hahnel

Foreword by Jeremy Brecher

South End Press
Cambridge, MA

Cover design by Ellen P. Shapiro
Globe Image Copyright © 1999 Photodisc, Inc.
Printed in Canada

Library of Congress Cataloging-in-Publication Data
Hahnel, Robin.
Panic rules! : everything you need to know about the global economy / by Robin Hahnel.
  p. cm.
Includes bibliographical references.
ISBN 0-89608-609-7. — ISBN 0-89608-610-0
1. Financial crises. 2. Business cycles. 3. International finance. 4. Social justice. 5. Economic policy. 6. Economic history—1945- . I. Title. II. Title: Guide to the global economic crisis. III. Title: Global economic crisis.
  HB3722.H34 1999   99-23928
  332'.042—dc21   CIP

South End Press, 7 Brookline Street, #1, Cambridge, MA 02139
04 03 02 01 00   2 3 4 5 6

There are two rules of behavior in any credit system.

Rule #1 is the rule all participants want all other participants to follow: DON'T PANIC!

Rule #2 is the rule each participant must be careful to follow herself: PANIC FIRST!

This book is dedicated to my five children:
Jesse, Ilana, Sara, Tanya, and Dylan

TABLE OF CONTENTS

ACKNOWLEDGMENTS

I especially thank Michael Albert and Lydia Sargent for urging me to write a series of articles for Z magazine on "Capitalist Globalism in Crisis," which appeared in December 1998 and January, February, March, and April 1999, and for encouraging me to expand upon those articles in this South End Press book. Without their persistence I would never have tackled the daunting task of interpreting the global crisis and evaluating reform proposals for a popular audience. I also thank Lynn Lu, my editor at South End Press, for her many valuable suggestions, as well as her enthusiasm and flexibility.

Discussions with Professors Cynthia Taft Morris, Colin Brandford, Maria Floro, and Dani Schydlowsky from American University and suggestions by Professor Peter Bohmer from Evergreen State University were especially helpful. But I am particularly indebted to Professor Robert Blecker, who has served as my mentor in international macroeconomics for more than a decade in the Political Economy program at American University, where we both teach.

Many students in my classes over the past three years have made helpful comments and suggestions, but three Ph.D. students who worked for me as research assistants deserve special thanks: Kristen Sheeran, Smita Wagh, and Ramya Mahadevanvijaya.

As much as I owe to those thanked above and others, the views expressed here are entirely my own responsibility.

FOREWORD
by Jeremy Brecher

A funny thing happened on the way to the New Millennium: the Old Millennium crashed. According to economist Paul Krugman, "Never in the course of economic events—not even in the early years of the Depression—has so large a part of the world economy experienced so devastating a fall from grace."

If you leaf back through the writings of mainstream economists and media pundits over the past decade, you will discover that such a global economic crisis couldn't happen, that it wasn't happening, that it wasn't as bad as people said, that it probably was a good thing in the long run, and that, anyway, it's over. If you want to escape this miasma of denial, read Robin Hahnel's *Panic Rules!*

In contrast to all the ballyhoo celebrating the "new global economy," Hahnel shows that for most people, globalization wasn't so cool even before this Pre-Millennial Meltdown. From 1980 to 1995, per capita GDP (Gross Domestic Product) grew less than 1 percent per year worldwide—with most of the gains going to the already rich. For every NIC (Newly Industrializing Country), there were ten of what Hahnel ironically dubs "FEBs"—countries Falling Evermore Behind. And for everyone growing wealthy on rising stock prices, profits, and high salaries, there were ten victims of downsizing and declining real wages.

Hahnel, himself an economist, challenges the economic dogma that unregulated markets, free trade, and globalization necessarily improve global economic efficiency, let alone that they must lead to benefits for all. Since the market doesn't charge firms for the environmental and social damage they do, unregulated markets give them an incentive to dump their wastes as cheaply as they can and to drive small farmers off the land, even if they then have to live in squalor in already bursting cities. Conversely, the market doesn't give individual firms an incentive to invest in education or health care, even if these are far more "efficient" means of creating well-being for society as a whole than producing sports utility vehicles.

Hahnel presents a theoretical case that, under free-trade conditions, even if there are "efficiency gains" from trade as each country specializes in what it does best, the lion's share of any gains from trade are likely to go to the wealthier trading partners, thereby aggravating global inequality. And in reality, this is just what has been happening in the era of globalization. A comparison of 56 countries shows that the spread in GDP per capita between the richest and poorest increased from 40:1 to 72:1 between 1973 and 1992. Just in the past four years, the world's 200 richest people have doubled their wealth, while the number of people living in absolute poverty has increased by 200 million.

When corporations and private wealth can move without regulation in the global free market, work forces, communities, and countries are forced to compete to attract footloose capital. The result has been called a "race to the bottom" in which environmental standards, social protections, and incomes are drawn down toward those of the poorest and most desperate. Hahnel shows that this was occurring even in globalization's boom phase.

Something else was happening, too: the accelerating growth of a global financial capital with little or no relation to the production of goods and services. New borrowing worldwide increased twentyfold from 1983 to 1998, while production only tripled. Daily trading in currency markets grew from $0.2 trillion in 1986 to $1.5 trillion in 1998. Less than 2 percent of that $1.5 trillion was used to finance international trade or investment in plant and capacity; an incredible 98 percent was for purely speculative activity. Trading in derivatives, perhaps the riskiest of all financial instruments, increased 215 percent per year between 1987 and 1997. By the time of the global meltdown in 1997, the value of derivatives traded during the year was more than ten times the total value of global production. It is this speculative "paper economy" that collapsed like a house of cards in 1997.

Officials from the U.S. and the IMF (International Monetary Fund) roamed the world, encouraging countries to "liberalize" their economies—to open them up to unrestricted flows of goods, services, and capital. One senior official in the U.S. Commerce Department recalled, "I never went on a trip when my brief didn't include either advice or congratulations on liberalization. We were convinced we were moving with the stream and that our job was to make the stream move faster. Wall Street was delighted." Speculative capital poured into so-called emerging markets: Investment by mutual funds in emerging markets, for example, increased from $1 billion in 1991 to $32 billion in 1996.

Trouble was, the money could pour out even faster than it poured in. Hahnel traces how an apparently local crisis in Thailand rapidly spread around the globe. In 1998, Thai GDP fell by 8 percent; in Indonesia it shrunk by 14 percent. There were roughly comparable declines in South Korea, Hong Kong, Malaysia, and Russia. In Indonesia, 20 million people lost their jobs in a year as the unemployment rate rose from less than 5 percent to more than 13 percent, and the number living in absolute poverty quadrupled to 100 million.

Faced with what threatened to become a global financial meltdown, the IMF rode to the "rescue." Oh, woe to those visited by such rescuers! In exchange for further loans, they imposed ruinous "conditionalities" under which countries had to raise interest rates, privatize public investments, open their economies to unlimited foreign ownership, cut social welfare, and rewrite their labor laws to eliminate workers' rights. The goal was to turn each stricken country into what Hahnel calls a "debt-repayment machine."

Hahnel quotes, of all people, conservative economist Milton Friedman saying that "IMF bailouts are hurting the countries they are lending to, and benefiting the foreigners who lend to them.... This is a different kind of foreign aid. It only goes through countries like Thailand to Bankers Trust." One example of the suffering caused by IMF "conditionalities": Oxfam International estimates that, in the Philippines alone, IMF-imposed cuts in preventative health care programs will result in 29,000 deaths from malaria and an increase of 90,000 in the number of untreated tuberculosis cases. Tribunals investigating "crimes against humanity," take note!

Business-page headlines proclaim that stocks have rebounded, currencies have recovered, and the crisis is therefore over. True, some stock markets and some currencies have rebounded, but 40 percent of the world remains in recession, and poverty continues to grow. And since the tidal waves of speculative capital sloshing around the world remain undiminished, a global meltdown remains a catastrophe just waiting to happen.

Meanwhile, global corporations based in the U.S. and Europe are gobbling up the economic resources of countries that have spent the past century struggling to escape from colonialism. A *Washington Post* article in late 1998 describes how "Hordes of foreign investors are flowing back into Thailand, boosting room rates at top Bangkok hotels despite the recession. Foreign investors have gone on a $6.7 billion shopping spree this year, snapping up bargain-basement steel mills, securities companies, supermarket chains, and other assets." And IMF "conditionalities" require that countries eliminate laws that might prevent this neocolonial asset grab. Perhaps this is one of the reasons that the world's 200 richest people have doubled their wealth in the past four years.

The economic mainstream is divided on what to do to prevent future meltdowns. What Hahnel dubs the "A Team"—a.k.a. free-traders, globalizers, or the Washington Consensus—calls for even more liberalization and even less "interference" with the workings of the market. An emerging "B Team," in contrast, is modernizing the ideas economist John Maynard Keynes developed in the Great Depression regarding the need for global financial regulation and coordinated fiscal and monetary policies worldwide in order to ward off economic meltdowns in the future.

The A Team's approach, according to Hahnel, is just what got us into the global mess in the first place. Some of the B Team's proposals could help stabilize the system, but without additional, more radical measures, they will also perpetuate the global economy's drive toward increasing inequality and environmental degradation. They only deserve support if they are combined with other measures that would actually reduce inequalities and environmental destruction—such as major debt relief for impoverished countries and price supports for third world exports.

When Hahnel presents his own alternatives, it is a shock to hear him, sounding like the most orthodox of economists, calling for more "global efficiency." But he makes clear that "efficiency" should not be equated with "profitability"—because private profit leaves out all those "external" costs and benefits that accrue to society as a whole rather than to wealth-holders. And he makes clear that environmental destruction is the most blatant kind of inefficiency. Instead, true efficiency requires that non-market institutions compensate for the "inefficient" biases of the market in order to "get prices right." He also points out that, in today's global economy, equity requires international cooperation to set non-market interest rates and terms of trade to distribute more of the benefits of globalization to the poorer economies. And Hahnel makes clear that "efficiency" should not be pursued at the expense of other values, like equity, democracy, diversity, solidarity, or environmental sustainability.

How are these goals to be achieved? Hahnel describes what has been called the "Lilliput Strategy," in which grassroots organizations, unions, and independent institutes and coalitions cooperate across national borders to contest the negative aspects of globalization. He points out that this approach has already won some important victories—such as the global grassroots campaign that recently blocked negotiation of the MAI (Multilateral Agreement on Investment), scotching what has been called a Magna Carta for global corporations. While the immediate objective of the Lilliput Strategy, Hahnel argues, should be to stop corporate-sponsored globalization in its tracks, it can and should also start the process of building a system of equitable international cooperation. Only in such a system can globalization provide the benefits that today it promises but in reality denies.

After describing the economic "A Team" and the "B Team," Hahnel states that "a C Team with a very different agenda and policies is needed." *Panic Rules!* provides the "C Team's" playbook.

INTRODUCTION

Walter Russell Mead provides a marvelous eyewitness account of how Asia caught the flu that is well worth quoting at length (*Esquire*, October 1998). Economists, politicians, and pundits have been arguing ever since about how all this could have happened.

It all began as a small cloud no bigger than a man's hand, quietly, the economic equivalent of a butterfly's wings in Beijing. There was a spot of trouble about the Thai baht—in itself, one of the world's more insignificant currencies. Pooh, pooh, said the experts as the rumors swirled. Thailand's a tiger; high savings rate, rapid economic growth, strong property market, strong banking sector. No problem, said the World Bank. Asia's cool, and Thailand's cool. The currency speculators thought differently. The baht had been linked to the dollar for more than a decade. Now that link looked weak. At 24 baht to the dollar, Thai exports looked expensive compared with products from places like China and Indonesia. Why not, a few speculators thought, bet against the baht for a while and see what happens? What happened was spectacular. The Thai central bank spent billions of dollars in a hopeless effort to defend its currency. By July of last year, the baht had fallen below 32 to the dollar, and it was taking the Thai economy down with it. I visited Bangkok soon after the baht crash, and parts of the city already looked like a ghost town. Work had stopped on dozens of skyscrapers; cranes were beginning to rust, and plastic sheeting was blowing off the sides of half-finished buildings. I checked out one of Bangkok's newest and most exclusive shopping malls, filled with Gucci and Versace vendors for the new generation of Thai yuppies. A piano player in a booth over the escalators put out bad late Elvis music as I cruised around the place. It looked like the sale of the century: signs everywhere advertised 70% discounts. But nobody except me and the piano player was there to look at them. The mall was empty.

The economists and the Asia experts were quick to reassure the world that the problem was limited to Thailand. Then a few rumors began to circulate about Malaysia. Ridiculous! the experts chorused together. Malaysia's economy wasn't weak like Thailand's, the experts pointed out. Malaysia wasn't corrupt, and the people were better educated. They were still giving speeches about how Malaysia would never go down when *crash!* The Malaysian ringgit joined the Thai baht on the ash heap of history. Malaysia's prime minister knew what to do: He blamed the Jews. They were jealous, it seems, of predominantly Muslim Malaysia's success.

The next round of rumors concerned Indonesia. Once again, the pundits, diplomats, and business leaders rallied as one. Too bad about the ringgit, said the experts. And sorry we were wrong about the baht. But now we understand. Malaysia had an erratic, some would say megalomaniacal, prime minister, too many expensive prestige projects, too much government interference with the credit system. And, of course, Thailand was more crooked than a Little Rock law firm. But Indonesia wasn't like that. Yes, there was corruption and injustice, but at least the Indonesian government—competent, thoughtful, focused on the economic fundamentals—got the macroeconomic policy right. Indonesia was no Thailand or Malaysia, they said. Let the baht and the ringgit sink to new lows; the rupiah was a stable currency supported by a sound economy. Then, of course, the rupiah crashed, going from about 2,500 to the dollar when I visited in August 1997 to as low as 16,000 in January. *Crash! Bang! Thump!* And just like that the rupiah took the Indonesian government with it. This time, the blame was on the Chinese rather than the Jews, and panicky mobs rioted through the streets of Indonesia's cities burning, looting, and raping ethnic Chinese who quickly moved to get as much of their money as possible out of the country, weakening the rupiah even further and making economic recovery more improbable.

After Indonesia, the line changed. Southeast Asia, the experts suddenly discovered, had never really been much of an economic success. Those years when the World Bank, the IMF, and the economics profession joined hands to sing hymns of praise to Southeast Asian governments and their solid economic policies were forgotten immediately. Southeast Asia, we now suddenly discovered, was full of paper tigers. Bad governments, uneducated people, unsophisticated technological bases, poorly functioning financial markets. The crisis was therefore contained; there was no danger that it could spread from such tiny, badly managed economies to bigger, more important, and better managed ones up north. Like, for example, South Korea, thank God. *Crash!* went the Korean won. I was there in January of this year; the won was in the toilet, the IMF was in charge of the economy, the demonstrators were in the streets, and I saw signs in Seoul store windows advertising something called an "IMF Sale": again, 70% off.

Singapore, they then reassured us, was well managed. *Crash!* said the Singapore dollar. Hong Kong was much more dynamic than all those state-planned economies, they said. *Crash!* went Hong Kong's stock market. Japan's been a little sluggish, but it is fundamentally sound, chorused the experts; Japan's got the largest foreign currency reserves in the world. *Crash!* answered the yen.

It was Lyndon Johnson's old nightmare: one Asian domino toppling after another—only it wasn't Communists pushing dominoes over but investors.

As the dominoes went down, the crisis shifted to the "Send in the Clowns" phase. Teams of IMF "experts" rushed into the capital cities to confer with political and business leaders. They then emerged for photo ops, brandishing what they said were recovery plans and multibillion-dollar bailouts. Sometimes within weeks, but certainly within months, they came crawling back. Sorry, the first bailout plan wasn't big enough, and the recovery plan isn't working. A few billion more, a few more tweaks to the plan, and then another photo op, followed in due course by new revelations that the bailout and the plan hadn't taken hold yet.

Up until July of 1997 we had been assured that the global economy had never been so virile as during the new era of global liberalization. We read in the 1997 *World Bank Report* that "the world economy grew at 3 percent a year in the 1980s and 2 percent in the first half of the 1990s," and that "low and middle income economies grew more rapidly, averaging 3.4 percent growth in the 1980s and 5 percent in the 1990s." In the same report we were told that "growth in trade from increased trade liberalization, increased private capital flows and financial integration, and internal privatization and progressive dismantling of regulations and controls" had produced a rising global economic tide that was lifting all but the most unseaworthy boats. And we have also been advised that since 43 percent of American households now own stocks, the spectacular increase in the U.S. stock market over the last decade has distributed generous benefits widely. But in Chapter 1 we will discover that the neoliberal economic "boom" that began in the early 1980s and ended in July 1997 was hardly what its admirers cracked it up to be. And in Chapter 3 we will discover that the "bust" in East Asia, which was soon followed by the Russian government default on its bonds, and "contagion" spreading the financial crisis to Brazil, has been even worse than most realize.

It is helpful to remember that among economic systems, capitalism is the manic-depressive patient. Exuberance, unbridled optimism, and euphoria—followed by gloom, listlessness, and depression—are the natural state of capitalist economies. But no matter how often the cycle is repeated, the patient always believes the latest boom will last forever, only to feel foolish again when the bubble bursts. And no matter how often the patient reverts to manic behavior when taken off medication, the economic "psychiatric" establishment eventually succumbs to the patient's pleas to be taken off medication during the "ups"—freeing the exuberant economy from policy restraints—only to rediscover that the patient must be put back on meds when the unmedicated manic "crashes."

The pattern has been repeated so often that two schools of thought have emerged within the "psychiatric" establishment known as mainstream economics. One school—the Neoliberal, Free Market "A Team"—proclaims the patient cured when its depression recedes, and proceeds to prescribe the dismantling of all restraints and regulations. Only when the patient once again "crashes" does pressure build for replacing the A Team with a different group of doctors from the Keynesian "B Team." The B Team specializes in policy restraints to fetter market euphoria, and strong anti-depressant medications to pull the economy out of its doldrums. The global economy has been under the care of the A Team since 1973, and it had begun to look as though the B Team had been permanently banned to the bullpen. But the East Asian crash, Russian default, and most importantly, continuing dangers that lurk in the international credit system that threaten the U.S. and European economies have B Teamers such as World Bank Chief Economist Joseph Stiglitz, MIT Professor Paul Krugman, and Harvard Institute for International Development Director Jeffrey Sachs warming up by lobbing pot-shots at prominent members of the A Team like U.S. Secretary of the Treasury Robert Rubin, Assistant Secretary of the Treasury Lawrence Summers, Federal Reserve Bank Chair Alan Greenspan, IMF Managing Director Michel Camdessus, and IMF Deputy Managing Director Stanley Fischer. This is the story line in the chapters that follow:

- All special characteristics of particular East Asian economies aside, the rapidly liberalized international credit system was an accident waiting to happen, and no minor adjustments in managing the global economy are going to put the genie of global financial wealth, which is now free to roam the planet at will, back into his bottle.

- The "boom" from 1980–97 was hardly an era of global prosperity, as neoliberals would have us believe. In fact, most people in the world were worse off economically at the end of the latest boom than they had been when it began—that is, even before it metamorphosed into the global economic crisis of 1997–99.

- Even *if* the International Keynesian B Team is put in charge, even *if* the B Team could put the credit crisis and the crisis in global demand back into their respective bottles—two very big "ifs"—globalization would continue to be a disaster for the global majority and the environment *unless* globalization is dramatically redirected.

- The A Team not only reflects an ideological predisposition toward leaving anything and everything to free markets, it represents the special interests of Western multinational corporations and particularly Western finance capital. The B Team not only reflects an ideological predisposition toward regulating markets, particularly in the financial sector, it represents the special interests of Western domestic and industrial capital. Neither team is ideologically opposed to corporate-sponsored globalization, which increases global inequality and environmental destruction. On the contrary, both the A and B Teams promote the kind of globalization that yields these results. They merely disagree about how best to facilitate this kind of globalization and whose interests within the corporate sector are to be most favored.

• Neither the A Team nor the B Team represents the interests of workers, peasants, and small business owners in either the first or third world—much less the interests of women, people of color, citizens of less developed economies, or the environment. Neither the A Team nor the B Team believes that globalization must be fundamentally redirected before it can reduce global inequality, promote economic democracy, and reduce environmental degradation. Therefore, a C Team with a very different agenda and policies is needed.

Recently the A Team troika of Alan Greenspan, Robert Rubin, and Lawrence Summers appeared on the cover of *Time* magazine, which dubbed them "The Committee to Save the World" (February 15, 1999). David Ignatius joked in the *Washington Post* that they are "the financial world's version of the Men in Black—vaporizing trade barriers here, bolstering currencies there, fending off what they regard as ill-considered European proposals for regulating exchange rates, and generally trying to keep the world financial system from spinning out of control." I'm sure that Joseph Stiglitz, Paul Krugman, and Jeffrey Sachs dream of the day when the B Team will appear on the cover of *Time*. I look forward to the more distant day when *Time* magazine—or will it be *Z* magazine?—displays a photo of the C Team on its cover. In my dream that photo contains the faces of hundreds of men and women representing a tiny sample of the tens of millions of faces of different colors and nationalities who are all spokespersons for the C Team. Under the photo in my dream the caption reads: "The People's Movement That Saved the World."

1   BLOOM OFF THE BOOM
The Facts

The truth is that neither part of the manic-depressive, boom-and-bust cycle of capitalism is "healthy." Like most capitalist booms, the benefits of global liberalization during the 1980s and 1990s were not all they were made out to be. In fact, most people in the world were worse off economically at the end of the latest boom in June 1997 than they had been when it began. How is this possible if the global economy grew, on average, 2.5 percent a year during the 1980s and 1990s, and if almost half of U.S. households are now stockholders?

First, world output grew more rapidly in the period *before* the great experiment in global deregulation than it has since. In the aftermath of World War II a number of international organizations were created at a conference held at Bretton Woods, New Hampshire. Besides the United Nations, the important international economic organizations created were the International Monetary Fund, or IMF, and the International Bank for Reconstruction and Development, now known as the World Bank. The IBRD-World Bank was established to help finance the reconstruction of war-torn Europe and the development of the poorer countries of the world. The IMF mandate was to regulate an international monetary system based on convertible currencies so as to facilitate global trade while leaving sovereign governments in charge of their own monetary, fiscal, and international investment policies. Significantly, the effort to establish the International Trade Organization, or ITO, ended in failure, leaving the "minimalist" General Agreement on Tariffs and Trade, or GATT, as its surviving remnant. But all that was more than 50 years

Table 1. Annual Average Rate of Growth of GDP Per Capita for 56 Countries

	1950–73	1973–92
12 Western European Countries	3.8%	1.8%
U.S.A., Canada, Australia, New Zealand	2.4%	1.2%
5 South European Countries	3.3%	2.6%
7 Eastern European Countries	4.0%	-0.8%
7 Latin American Countries	2.4%	0.4%
11 Asian Countries	3.1%	3.5%
10 African Countries	1.8%	-0.4%

Source: Angus Maddison, *Monitoring the World Economy 1820–1992,* OECD 1995.

ago. While changes in the system have been continuous, 1973 is considered the end of the Bretton Woods "era" and beginning of the neoliberal "era" of deregulation and in particular removal of restrictions on the movement of capital across international borders. Table 1 gives the average annual rates of growth of GDP per capita for 56 countries during the two eras.

Admittedly, this is a "crude" comparison between a single cause and its supposed result. Nonetheless, it should be apparent why the Bretton Woods era of international controls and interventions, 1950–73, is referred to as the "golden era of capitalism," and the neoliberal era of international deregulation, 1973–92, is not. If there had truly been efficiency gains from global deregulation, would they not have shown up as higher rates of growth? Instead we see significant declines in the rate of growth of per capita GDP for every region in the world except Asia, where the growth rate increased slightly during the era of liberalization. Moreover, the Asian "miracle" was most notable in economies that pursued the "Asian development model," which was the antithesis of laissez-faire. Governments in the Asian tigers actively deployed differential tax and credit policies in accord with a planned pattern of industrialization and trade. Of course, there are many reasons other than international liberalization that may have reduced economic growth over the past quarter-century, but the above figures hardly suggest significant efficiency gains from international liberalization. And remember, we are only comparing the neoliberal era *before* the bubble burst in 1997 with the Bretton Woods era.

Second, world population grew along with GDP from 1980 to 1995. While world GDP grew at an annual rate of roughly 2.5 percent, world population grew at 1.6 percent per year over the same period, leaving less than a 1 percent annual increase in per capita GDP over the period. *Third,* GDP is a notorious overestimate of the benefits from economic activity. The work of environmental economists such as Herman Daly and John Cobb Jr., James Tobin and William Nordhaus, Roberto Reppeto,[1] and others suggests that when depreciation of produced *and* natural capital is subtracted, and when environmental degradation is accounted for, what at first appears to have been a meager annual increase in economic well-being per person may even have been a *decrease* in average sustainable well-being per capita during our most recent stretch of "good times." *Fourth,* corrections due to "green accounting"—which simply apply the same treatment to natural capital as to human-made capital, and to environmental amenities as to other goods and services—do *not* account for adverse changes in the distribution of income or increases in economic insecurity. Yet, along with the increased pace of environmental degradation, rising inequality of income and wealth, and increasing economic insecurity were far and away the most significant features of the neoliberal "good years" we enjoyed—before the Asian crisis struck in 1997.

Economist Henry Aaron, veteran analyst of income distribution for the Brookings Institution, remarked in 1978 that looking for changes in U.S. income distribution "was like watching the grass grow." That has most emphatically not been the case since 1980. In the U.S. the share of income of the top 5 percent of households climbed from 16.6 percent of all income in 1973 to 21.2 percent in 1994.[2] The share of the richest 20 percent rose from 43.6 percent to 49.1 percent, while the share of the poorest 20 percent fell from 4.2 percent to 3.5 percent. Worse still, not only has the relative share of income fallen among the bottom half of the income distribution in the U.S., but their absolute income has fallen as well. The average income of the poorest 20 percent fell by 2.7 percent between 1973 and 1994, and that of the second poorest 20 percent fell by 3.8 percent, while that of the top 20 percent rose by 27.2 percent and that of the top 5 percent rose by a dramatic 44.2 percent. A statistic called the Gini coefficient is the most commonly used measure of inequality. In any distribution, perfect equality yields a Gini coefficient of zero while perfect inequality yields a Gini coefficient of one. The Gini coefficient measuring income inequality in the U.S. rose from 0.419 to 0.479 between 1975 and 1993—more than a 14 percent increase in inequality.

The increase in wealth inequality in the U.S. was even more dramatic than the increase in income inequality during the neoliberal "good times." The share of total wealth owned by the top 1 percent almost doubled between 1976 and 1992. This was largely because the top 1 percent of wealth-holders received 62 percent of the total gain in wealth between 1983 and 1989, while the bottom 80 percent got only 1 percent of the new wealth over that period. Worse still, the average wealth of the bottom 40 percent of wealth-holders actually declined. Meanwhile, the average real wage in the U.S. fell by 11 percent between 1973 and 1993 despite continued increases in labor productivity, with the largest drops occurring in the lower wage brackets. In contrast, corporate profit rates in the U.S. in 1996 reached their highest level since these data were first collected in 1959. And while it is true that 43 percent of U.S. households now own stocks, since most own very little, largely through 401(K) and other retirement accounts, the top 10 percent of households has appropriated 86 percent of the stock market gains since 1989.

In a major article, "Cross-National Comparisons of Earnings and Income Inequality," published in the *Journal of Economic Literature* in June 1997, Peter Gottschalk and Timothy Smeeding reviewed a large body of literature that showed that rising income inequality since 1980 was not limited to the U.S. They concluded:

> Increases in the dispersion of both individual earnings and total household income in the United States were larger than in almost all other OECD countries. However, the United States was not the only advanced economy to experience an increase in inequality during the 1980s and early 1990s.

Most OECD countries experienced at least modest increases in earnings and market income inequality.

Experts are unanimous that significant increases in earnings inequality characterize the neoliberal period from 1980 to the present throughout the developed world. Three years ago the disparity between official figures indicating significant, sustained economic growth in the U.S. and surveys revealing that most Americans feared more for their economic futures than at any time since the Great Depression gave rise to a surprising seven-part series in the *New York Times* on "downsizing" (March 1–7, 1999). The *Times* series kindled so much interest that other major dailies, like the *Washington Post* and *Los Angeles Times,* scurried to print their own imitations. As layoffs extended from blue-collar workers to middle management and from rust-belt industries to financial services, as the number of Americans with no health care insurance climbed to 43.4 million, as temporary and part-time jobs replaced permanent full-time jobs, as low-skill, low-wage jobs replaced high-skill, high-wage jobs, as hours worked per family climbed while most family incomes stagnated, the discrepancy between rising economic fortunes for the few and declining economic conditions for most had finally became impossible for even the *Times* and fellow travelers to ignore completely. But three more years of low unemployment and inflation, coupled with a spectacular run on the U.S. stock market, allowed the media to replace stories about family tragedies from downsizing with exhilarating stock market updates, effectively silencing the alarm bell. Only recently, as clouds have appeared on the international economic horizon, threatening the Wall Street bubble, have pundits begun to ask themselves if it was wise to ignore earlier warning signals.

Just as the boom increased inequality within the U.S. and to a lesser extent in other developed economies, the boom increased per capita income differences between countries. Economists Walter Park and David Brat of American University calculated that the Gini coefficient for GDP per capita in 91 countries for which data were available rose steadily throughout the neoliberal "boom." [3] Regional disparities also increased. Latin America did not share in the boom during the "lost decade" of the 1980s, as those countries suffered through their debt crisis. The boom bypassed the Middle East and Northern Africa as oil prices sagged. It completely passed over sub-Saharan Africa as their terms of trade deteriorated along with their natural capital. And even before the latest debacle in Russia, no boom appeared to reward those who embraced capitalism in Eastern Europe and the countries of the former Soviet Union after the "fall of the wall." Listed alphabetically, *annual* average growth rates for those economies from 1990 through 1995— *before* the "crisis" in "emerging markets"—were as follows:

Table 2. Annual Average Rate of Growth of GDP for Post-Communist Economies

Armenia	-21.2%	Latvia	-13.7%
Azerbaijan	-20.2%	Lithuania	-9.7%
Belarus	-9.3%	Poland	+2.4%
Bulgaria	-4.3%	Romania	-1.4%
Czech Republic	-2.6%	Russian Federation	-9.8%
Estonia	-9.2%	Slovak Republic	-2.8%
Georgia	-26.9%	Tajikistan	-18.1%
Hungary	-1.0%	Turkmenistan	-10.6%
Kazakstan	-11.9%	Ukraine	-14.3%
Kyrgyz Republic	-14.7%	Uzbekistan	-4.4%

Source: World Bank, 1997.

The case of Russia is the best known. After five years of IMF-led economic "reform," Russians have lost about half of their national income, and now per capita income in Russia is only a little more than *half* as much as income per capita in Mexico! Unemployment rates are meaningless, since millions of workers who are officially employed are not being paid. Life expectancy for males plummeted from 65.6 years to 57 years in only five years—even before the latest collapse of the rouble, government and private sector default, and cessation of IMF loan disbursements.

Table 3. Annual Average Rate of Growth of GDP for East Asian "Tigers"

	1980–89	1990–95
China	+10.2%	+12.8%
Hong Kong	+6.9%	+5.6%
Indonesia	+6.1%	+7.6%
Korean Republic	+9.4%	+7.2%
Malaysia	+5.2%	+8.7%
Singapore	+6.4%	+8.7%
Thailand	+7.6%	+8.4%

Source: World Bank, 1997.

In fact, other than the most wealthy in the U.S., the benefits of deregulation and globalization passed over pretty much everyone except those in East Asia. And since the largest economy in East Asia, Japan, was stagnant throughout the 1990s, the boom was actually much more specific to a few East Asian countries. In Table 3, the first figure is the *annual* average growth of GDP from 1980 through 1989, the second is the *annual* average growth of GDP from 1990 through 1995 for the East Asian "tigers." This is not only a remarkable performance, but a remarkable list. With the single exception of China, every East Asian "success story"—which *is,* essentially, the entire neoliberal "boom" we are supposed to be awed by—is now on the endangered economy species list since the "bust" of 1997–98.

At this point a slight digression on China is necessary. There is little doubt that China has so far been spared the fate of its fellow East Asian tigers largely because its totalitarian political regime resisted international pressure to make the yuan a convertible currency and remove all controls on international capital flows—even while the Chinese leadership hastened the spread of capitalism internally and aggressively pursued an export-led growth strategy. But I don't believe the numbers. If true, 16 years of annual growth rates well over 10 percent in an economy of a billion people would be a remarkable economic success story. It would be remarkable even if accompanied by significant environmental deterioration and by the most dramatic increase in economic inequality in any country in modern world history—which is likely the case. But while the figures on growth of output are published by the World Bank, the raw numbers, as is the case for all countries, are provided by the government of the country. Chinese government economic statistics have long been subject to political manipulation—more so than in the case of any other country of which I am aware. There were times when Chinese Communist leaders so mistrusted their own government figures on Chinese agricultural production, for example, that they instead used CIA data collected from spy satellites for making policy decisions. Moreover, the political allies of former Party boss Deng Xiaoping, who have run China throughout this period, are the most notorious falsifiers of information for political expediency from the old Communist Party.

But the reported growth rates are *so big,* how could they possibly be making the whole thing up? I don't think the figures are entirely fictitious, but I suspect they are very misleading even when not fictitious. I suspect that the prices used to evaluate the output of goods and services whose output has stagnated or declined—such as basic grains—are seriously undervalued, while the prices of goods whose output has increased—like meat, garden vegetables, and commercial real estate—are greatly overvalued. I also suspect that many goods and services provided to employees and their families by state enterprises, which were not counted before, are now being counted as they are produced for profit. I mention these doubts because, if I am correct, much of what appears to be an economic miracle in China may never have happened—in which case the miracle of liberalized globalization from 1980 to 1996 reduces to short-lived success stories in a handful of East Asian economies accompanied by a regressive redistribution of wealth and income in a handful of advanced economies.

As best I can tell, for every NIC (Newly Industrializing Country) there were 10 FEBs (countries Falling Ever-more Behind) during the neoliberal "boom." And for every wealthy beneficiary of rising stock prices, rising profit shares, and rising high-end salaries, there were 10 victims of declining real wages, decreased job security, and lost benefits. The recent experiment in deregulation and globalization was indeed both "the best of times and the worst of times." But unfortunately it was the best of times for only a few, and the worst of times for most. At least that is what had been happening *before* the bubble burst in July 1997.

Notes

1. See Daly and Cobb, *For the Common Good* (Boston: Beacon Press, 1989); Nordhaus and Tobin, "Is Growth Obsolete?" in *Economic Growth, Fiftieth Anniversary Colloquium*, Vol. 5 (Cambridge, MA: National Bureau of Economic Research, 1972); and Reppeto, *Wasting Assets* (Washington, DC: World Resources Institute, 1989).

2. The figures below are taken from Edward Nathan Wolff, *Economics of Poverty, Inequality and Discrimination* (Cincinnati, OH: South-Western Publishing Co., 1997).

3. Walter Park and David Brat, "A Global Kuznets Curve?" in *Kylos*, Vol. 48, 1995.

2   DECONSTRUCTING THE NEOLIBERAL MYTH
Analysis

Not even the most rabid neoliberals claim that international liberalization and deregulation have reduced global inequality or slowed the pace of environmental degradation. But neoliberals do claim that whatever other harm they may have caused, international liberalization and deregulation *must have* produced efficiency gains. Unfortunately, as we saw in Chapter 1, this picture does not fit the facts. Growth of world GDP per capita was significantly lower during the neoliberal era than the Bretton Woods era, which was characterized by international controls and interventions. And except for the wealthy in the U.S. and a handful of East Asian economies whose governments largely forswore the laissez-faire philosophy, most of the world's citizens were worse off in 1996 than they had been at the end of the 1970s. Why did global liberalization fail to yield efficiency gains, and why, despite strong evidence to the contrary, do most economists insist that it must?

Alan Greenspan reiterated this view most recently in a speech in Dallas. John Berry reported on April 17, 1999, in the *Washington Post* under the title "Fed Chief Backs Free Trade":

> Federal Reserve Chairman Alan Greenspan, arguing that free trade raises living standards, yesterday deplored recent politically driven actions to protect various industries from foreign competition. "The United States has been in the forefront of the postwar opening up of international markets, much to our, and the rest of the world's, benefit. It would be a great tragedy were that process reversed."

Reuters News Service quoted the Chairman's remarks in Dallas at greater length:

> If trade barriers are lowered by both parties, each clearly benefits. But if one lowers barriers and the other does not, the country that lowered barriers unilaterally would still be better off having done so. I regret that trade policy has been inextricably linked with job creation. We try to promote free trade on the mistaken ground that it will create jobs. The reason should be that it enhances standards of living through the effects of competition on productivity.

Belief in the benefits of international trade and investment is one of the most sacred convictions of economists. To question the existence of efficiency gains from specialization and trade is tantamount to a confession of economic illiteracy in professional circles. Before proceeding to explain why further liberalization of international trade and investment are likely to continue to increase global inequality and environmental degradation, let me explain why they may even fail to produce efficiency gains.

Are There Always Gains from Trade?

It is illogical to deny that if the true social opportunity costs of producing goods are different in different countries, there are potential efficiency gains from specialization and trade. (See Appendix A for an explanation of "opportunity costs" and their relevance to trade and efficiency.) And it is illogical to deny that if there are efficiency gains, it is *theoretically* possible to distribute them so as to reduce global inequality and/or environmental degradation. After all, an efficiency gain is an efficiency gain, and *theoretically* could be "spent" any way we choose—including on poverty reduction or environmental restoration. The theory of Comparative Advantage (CA) is logically sound when it teaches that whenever opportunity costs differ between countries, each country *could* be made better off by specializing in the production of the good for which its opportunity cost of production is lower and trading for the good for which its opportunity cost of production is higher. CA theory is also logically sound when it teaches that the range of mutually beneficial terms of trade is defined by the different opportunity costs in the trading countries. Finally, CA theory correctly teaches that the closer the terms of trade to the opportunity cost in Country 1, the greater the share of the efficiency gain from specialization and trade that goes to Country 2; and the closer the terms of trade to the opportunity cost in Country 2, the greater the share of the efficiency gain from specialization and trade that goes to Country 1. Appendix A contains an explanation of the theory of comparative advantage that is the centerpiece of mainstream trade theory, and a demonstration of these results. But what CA theory does *not* speak to is where in the range of feasible terms of trade the actual terms of trade will end up. Therefore what CA theory tells us *nothing* about is how the efficiency gain from specialization and trade will be divided between the two countries. If the lion's share of the benefit goes to the country that is worse off, global inequality would be reduced by trade. But if the lion's share of the efficiency gain from specialization and trade goes to the country that was better off in the first place, global inequality will be increased by trade. In other words, CA theory simply does not speak to the question of whether trade will result in more or less economic inequality among countries—an issue that should be central to our concerns—so we have to look to theories beyond CA to address this deficiency.

Similarly, it is illogical to deny that if the social productivity of capital differs in different countries, there are potential efficiency gains from international lending, and these gains could *theoretically* be used to advance any cause. By reallocating capital from countries where it is less socially productive to ones where it is more socially productive, we achieve an efficiency gain. Of course, how this efficiency gain will be distributed depends on the interest rate on international loans. Any interest rate higher than the productivity of capital in the lending country but lower than the productivity of capital in the borrowing country will distribute benefits to both countries. If international interest rates were closer to the opportunity cost of capital in lending countries, the lion's share of the benefit would go to borrowing countries and would thereby diminish global inequality. But when international interest rates are closer to the opportunity cost of capital in borrowing countries, lending countries capture the lion's share of the efficiency gain, and global inequality rises.

Now that we have "rendered unto Caesar what is Caesar's," let me make clear what should not be conceded to mainstream trade theory. The usual statements and interpretations of the above propositions do not follow from what I have just conceded. It does not follow from the existence of different social opportunity costs in different countries that trade *necessarily* yields efficiency gains. And it does not follow from the fact that the social productivity of capital differs in different countries that international lending *necessarily* yields efficiency gains.

First, what if more trade or international investment leads to more global disequilibrium, and the efficiency loss from unemployed resources outweighs the efficiency gain from their greater productivity once they are redeployed? Mainstream theoretical economists concede this point, but mainstream practitioners invariably ignore it. Specialization and trade mean shifting labor and resources between industries and, frequently, locations. Unemployed workers and underutilized factory capacity, retraining expenses, and any costs of building social infrastructure, like schools and roads, in new locations when expanding industries are in different cities and regions from contracting industries are all efficiency losses that might outweigh any efficiency gains from increased trade. Similarly, it is now apparent to those living in East Asian economies that more international lending can result in financial crises when speculative bubbles burst, leading, in turn, to reductions in investment, production, and employment capable of wiping out strong growth during decades in only a year or two of severe economic crisis.

Second, what if prices are "wrong," that is, what if they do not accurately reflect the true social opportunity costs of traded goods or capital? In this case trade based on prices different from social opportunity costs might produce efficiency losses, even if trade based on accurate opportunity costs *would* produce efficiency gains. Again, any mainstream theoretician will concede the point when it is put this way. But few mainstream economists have ever considered that market prices may differ from true social opportunity costs by, say, 30 percent or more, and that a significant degree of "miss-signaling" could yield trade that results in counterproductive patterns of specialization.

For instance, what if the social costs of modern agricultural production in the U.S. are far greater than the private costs because environmentally destructive effects such as soil erosion and pesticide run-off go uncounted—as many environmentalists believe? And what if life in traditional Mexican villages has significant advantages vis-à-vis disease prevention and effective community social safety nets compared with life in Mexican urban slums—as many social workers testify? In this case it is quite possible that trading Mexican shoes for U.S. grain based on comparative *private* advantage, which moves Mexican peasants from rural agriculture to shoe factories in Mexico City and transfers productive resources in the U.S. from shoe factories to modern agriculture, may lower, not raise, economic efficiency. In this case, miss-signaling in the price system could generate efficiency losses, not gains, from liberalized trade under NAFTA—even in the absence of unemployment effects.

Similarly, it is *possible* that if interest rates do not reflect the true social opportunity cost of capital in different countries, or if international credit markets divert lending from productive to speculative uses, credit liberalization *might* produce efficiency losses rather than gains. Since interest rates in a country reflect the bargaining power between labor and capital, the bargaining power between finance and industrial capital, and the policy decisions of monetary authorities as well as the social opportunity cost of capital, there is good reason to fear that interest rates can miss-signal. If liberalization of international financial markets ties up more capital in short-run speculation in currencies, bonds, and stocks, leaving less available for long-term business loans to increase productive capacity, global production might fall, not rise, with an increase in international lending. In 1980 daily transactions in international currency markets totaled only $80 billion. By 1995 $1.26 trillion was exchanged in currency markets per day. And today more than $1.5 trillion changes hands daily in currency markets. Even if we assume that any foreign exchange transactions carried out to finance international trade or business investment in plant and capacity are productive, less than 2 percent of the more than $1.5 trillion is going to productive purposes, meaning that more than 98 percent is being siphoned off into purely speculative activity!

Trade, Investment, and Global Inequality
Even if prices did not miss-signal, and even if markets equilibrated instantaneously—two very big "ifs"—and therefore a more efficient international use of productive resources resulted from international trade and investment, it is disingenuous to be "agnostic" regarding the likely distributive effects of international trade and invest-

ment, as mainstream theorists invariably are. The interested reader should consult Appendix B for a simple but powerful model that illustrates the following result: As long as capital is scarce globally, there is good reason to expect that international trade *based on free-market prices* will distribute more of the efficiency gains to wealthier countries than to poorer countries and thereby increase global inequality. And it is even easier to demonstrate that if capital is scarce globally, there is every reason to expect that *free-market interest rates* will increase global inequality by distributing more of the efficiency gains from international investment to wealthier lenders than to poorer borrowers.

In other words, even if there are gains in global efficiency from liberalization of trade and investment, and even if there are gains in absolute terms for poorer as well as wealthier economies, we should expect the gap between rich and poor countries to widen as a result of international liberalization under free-market conditions. The international terms of trade and interest rates are what determine how efficiency gains are distributed between countries. While it is possible to choose terms of trade and international interest rates that *would* reduce global inequality, if capital is scarce relative to labor *globally,* models like the one in Appendix B demonstrate why there is every reason to expect free-market terms of trade and free-market interest rates to distribute the lion's share of any efficiency gains to countries that were wealthier in the first place. So there is no reason to be surprised when data on global inequality reveal that this is what has occurred.

Between 1950 and 1973, when expansion of trade and international investment was slower, the spread between GDP per capita in the richest and poorest of the seven *regions* listed in Table 1 (see Chapter 1) increased only from 10:1 to 11:1. But between 1973 and 1992, when trade and international investment expanded dramatically, the spread increased from 11:1 to 16:1. The spread between the richest and poorest of the 56 *countries* included in Table 1 increased only from 35:1 to 40:1 between 1950 and 1973, but between 1973 and 1992, the spread increased from 40:1 to 72:1.

Second, it is likely that liberalization of international trade and credit will affect wage, interest, and profit rates within countries in ways that increase internal inequalities. While mainstream trade theory disguises the possibility of efficiency losses from trade, as well as the likelihood of inegalitarian distributive effects *between* countries, at least one pillar of mainstream trade theory from two Scandinavian economists, Eli Heckscher and Bertil Ohlin, helps us understand the likelihood of inegalitarian internal effects. According to Heckscher-Ohlin theory, if trade actually does generate efficiency gains, it will be because it leads countries to specialize in the production of goods in which they have a comparative advantage, which will tend to be those goods that use inputs, or factors of production, in which the country is relatively abundant. But this means trade increases the demand for relatively abundant factors of production and decreases the demand for relatively scarce factors within countries. In advanced economies where the capital-labor ratio is higher than in third world economies and therefore capital is "relatively abundant," Heckscher-Ohlin theory predicts that increased trade will increase the demand for capital, increasing its return, and decrease the demand for labor, depressing wages—as has, in fact, occurred in the U.S., making the AFL-CIO a consistent critic of trade liberalization. In advanced economies where the ratio of skilled to unskilled labor is higher than in third world economies, Heckscher-Ohlin theory also predicts that increased trade will increase the demand for skilled labor and decrease the demand for unskilled labor and thereby increase wage differentials. In a study published by the pro-globalization Institute for International Economics in 1997, William Cline estimates that 39 percent of the increase in wage inequality in the U.S. over the past 20 years was due solely to increased trade.

On the other hand, the internal distributive effects of international trade within third world economies predicted by Heckscher-Ohlin deserve serious consideration by progressives. In third world economies where labor is relatively abundant and capital is relatively scarce, and unskilled labor is relatively abundant and skilled labor is relatively scarce, Heckscher-Ohlin theory predicts that increased trade *should* cause wages to rise and the return to capital to fall, and *should* reduce the wage differential between skilled and unskilled labor. In other words, while Heckscher-Ohlin predicts that international trade will aggravate inequalities within the advanced economies, it predicts that international trade will reduce inequalities within third world economies. Since it is undeniable that unskilled third world residents are the most economically needy of all earth's citizens, this issue deserves important consideration. Indeed, proponents of free trade in the U.S. often throw this argument in the face of those who oppose globalization, accusing us of favoring workers in the advanced economies at the expense of workers, and particularly the least-skilled workers, in underdeveloped economies. *Are we guilty?*

First of all, Heckscher-Ohlin theory says nothing about the distribution of the benefits of trade *between* countries. Their theory is silent on this subject, as all mainstream theory is. But we have seen that as long as capital is scarce relative to labor globally, the lion's share of the benefits from expanded trade under free-market conditions will in all likelihood be captured by the more advanced economies, thereby increasing global inequality. In which case, even if third world wages were increased by expanded trade, as Heckscher-Ohlin predicts, third world workers would be expanding their share of an economic pie that is shrinking relative to the economic pie of the advanced economies. But is it really true that trade liberalization is likely to boost wages within third world economies?

Heckscher and Ohlin's logic is impeccable, but theories are based on assumptions that sometimes do not hold in the real world. First of all, Heckscher-Ohlin theory does *not* predict that increased demand for labor will raise wages if the supply of labor is infinitely elastic. Many development economists, starting with Arthur Lewis, have argued that labor is often in such great oversupply in many third world economies that increased demand for labor expands employment but fails to raise wages, meaning that the supply of labor *is* almost infinitely elastic. But the fact is, we are *not* guilty of caring more about workers in advanced economies than unskilled third world residents when we oppose globalization for another reason as well. The combination of the so-called green revolution in agriculture and economic globalization is destroying traditional agriculture in third world economies. Before the spread of "modern" agricultural techniques, the rise of multinational agribusiness, and the emergence of global agricultural markets, large amounts of land in the third world had a sufficiently low value to permit billions to live on it, producing mostly for their own consumption even though their productivity was quite low. Globalization and modern agriculture for export have raised the value of that land. Peasant squatters are no longer tolerated. Peasant renters are thrown off by owners who want to use the land for more valuable export crops. Even peasants who own their family plots fall easy prey to local economic and political elites who now see a far more valuable use for that land and have become much more aggressive land-grabbers through all sorts of legal and extralegal means. And finally, as third world governments relax restrictions on foreign ownership of land, local land sharks are joined by multinational agribusinesses, adding to the human exodus. Globalization has already thrown hundreds of millions of peasants off land where they made a poor living, to be sure, but were nonetheless better off than they now are, living in disease-infested slums surrounding swollen third world cities where productive employment is even less likely than it was in their rural villages, and where traditional social safety nets are nonexistent. And unless globalization is stopped, or its character fundamentally changed, it will soon be billions who travel this "trail of tears," adding to the supply of urban unemployed whose reservation wage has dropped from the very low average productivity of labor in traditional agriculture to literally zero.

The relevance of this to Heckscher-Ohlin theory is that the increase in the supply of urban labor caused by the ruin of traditional third world agriculture may well dwarf any increase in the demand for third world labor from increased specialization in the production of labor-intensive manufactured exports (or more direct foreign investment). In other words, the rural-to-urban migration effect of globalization resulting from the destruction of traditional agriculture may swamp the Heckscher-Ohlin effect on returns to relatively abundant factors of production in most third world economies. In which case, the net result would be greater un-employment and lower wages—particularly for those who were already the "wretched of the earth."

Free-Market Globalization and the Environment

Mainstream theory starts from the presumption that global liberalization increases global economic growth and then proceeds to channel our thinking about the relationship between the international economy and the environment into two competing theories about the relationship between economic growth and the environment. The Doomsday theories say the more goods and services we produce per capita, the greater the strain we put on the environment per person because we deplete our "natural capital" and degrade our environment with waste. The Pollyanna theories say that as per capita income increases, more people will choose to spend to protect and preserve the environment since consumers' demand for "environmental amenities" should increase with income. While there is more to be learned from the first theory than the second, there is plenty wrong with both theories. But the sleight of hand is in framing the debate in this way.

The real issue is not the relationship between growth in the value of the goods and services produced per person (and therefore income per capita) and the environment, but how to change the mix of goods and services we consume, and the technologies we use to produce them, so that the difference between the benefits people enjoy and the burdens they suffer from their economic activities increases while damaging the environment less. In other words, "Growth of *what?*" and "Produced *how?*" are more important questions for the environment than "*How much* growth?" And therefore, the relevant question to ask about international trade and investment under free-market conditions is whether it aids or hinders the process of changing our consumption basket and production technologies in environmentally friendly ways. There are at least four reasons free-market capitalist globalization leads us to consume a mixture of goods and services and to produce them in ways that inefficiently misuse the environment—independent of the relationship between growth and the environment per se.

- To a great extent the natural environment is a "common property resource," and when users motivated by individual concerns have "free access," they predictably "overexploit" common property resources.

If all users have free access to a resource, standard economic theory teaches us that they will use that resource more intensively than is socially efficient because individual users have no reason to take into account two negative effects that their use has on others: (1) The more each uses the resource this year, the less benefit others who also use the resource this year will obtain for their efforts. (2) The more of the resource each uses this year, the less of the resource will be available for anyone to use in future years. Oceans, waterways, and the atmosphere are for the most part "common property resources," which standard theory predicts will be "overexploited" under a system of free access. As long as globalization makes more of the environment more free for more users to exploit, the degree of overexploitation will be greater.

Moreover, a solution to overexploitation of common property resources is to substitute for the system of free access some collective system of management that successfully limits use. In her exhaustive study of common property resource systems all over the world—both successful and unsuccessful—titled *Governing the Commons* (Cambridge University Press, 1990), economist Elnor Ostrom concludes that the most critical factor to establishing and maintaining successful democratic systems of common property management is a stable population of users who also have many other relationships with one another. Unfortunately, the current form of globalization is anathema to the kind of community stability Ostrom assures us is most important for preventing overexploitation of our common property environmental resources.

- Pollution is a "negative externality" of production or consumption activity. Since market economies predictably overproduce goods and services whose production or consumption entails negative external effects—since buyers and sellers have no incentive to take those negative effects *on others* into account— they also produce more pollution than is economically efficient.

Free-market globalization not only brings more decisions about what to produce and how to produce it into the market decision-making system—thereby leading to more pollution than is efficient even by the most conservative standards; global capital mobility forces countries to "compete" with one another for business investment by reducing emissions taxes and quotas, lowering fines, and reducing funds for monitoring, i.e., by cutting back on policies designed to partially correct for this predictable inefficiency of the market system. Jeremy Brecher calls the effects on environmental regulation part of the "race to the bottom" unleashed by increased capital mobility.

- Pollution reduction is a "public good," and, due to the "free rider problem" and "transaction costs," market economies underproduce public goods in general, and pollution reduction in particular.

There is an incentive for everyone who benefits from a public good to try to avoid paying the cost of providing the good, and instead "ride for free" on others' purchases. When someone else buys a private good, I do not benefit. But when others buy a public good, I can benefit as much as they do. Since everyone benefits from pollution reduction, and no one can be excluded from the benefits of pollution reduction, pollution reduction is a public good. And just like any public good, pollution reduction will be underdemanded, and therefore underproduced in the context of market incentives. Since the current globalization is principally an expansion of market incentives, we should expect less pollution reduction as a result.

Increased greenhouse gas emissions, deforestation, and resulting climate change illustrate both of the last two reasons markets are destroying the environment. Human economic activity over the past 100 years has led to dramatic increases in atmospheric concentrations of carbon dioxide. Between 1860 and 1990 global carbon emissions rose from less than 200 million to almost 6 billion metric tons per year. At the same time, deforestation has considerably reduced the recycling of carbon dioxide into oxygen. The combined result of increased carbon emissions and reduced sequestration is an increase in the stock of greenhouse gases in the atmosphere to the point of climate change with serious adverse affects. At its old steady state level the greenhouse effect was making the earth inhabitable—preventing the earth's mean temperature from falling well below freezing and reducing temperature fluctuation between day and night. But higher levels of greenhouse gases in the atmosphere mean global temperatures will rise and extreme climate conditions will intensify. Droughts will be longer, floods more severe, and hurricanes and tornadoes more frequent; melting polar ice caps will raise sea levels and threaten a large percentage of the world's population that lives in coastal cities.

This is happening in large part because businesses and households that burn fossil fuels are not charged for the adverse effect their actions have on the atmosphere—carbon emissions are a negative externality. The energy and transportation systems we have are not the only energy and transportation systems that could have accompanied economic growth, or even industrialization, during the past two centuries. Energy and transportation systems based on burning fossil fuels are largely the product of a market system that systematically failed to charge users of fossil fuels for the full costs of their use (and of a Communist system that mindlessly aped that market system). Furthermore, global warming is accelerating because owners or users of tropical forests are not paid for the beneficial effect of carbon sequestration if they choose to preserve the forests intact—carbon sequestration is a positive externality.[*] Markets lead us to engage in too many activities

---

[*] Tropical forests sequester carbon dioxide more efficiently than forests in temperate climates because the species and density of flora are better suited to sequestration, and also because sequestration is enhanced by warmer temperatures. So the focus on destruction of tropical forests is warranted on scientific grounds. However, northern forests provide sequestration and other valuable environmental services as well, and their devastation has

with negative external effects and too few activities with positive external effects. Hence, too much fossil fuel burning and too little forest preservation occur under market incentives.

Moreover, reductions in carbon emissions are public goods, as is the preservation of forests that convert carbon dioxide back into oxygen. But since no one can be excluded from benefiting from these public goods, and each entails private sacrifices, all businesses, consumers, and nations will wait for someone else to shoulder the burden of providing the public good in hopes of riding for free on others' sacrifices. Every country wants to enjoy the benefits associated with carbon-emitting activity and hopes others will reduce their carbon emissions. It is not hard to see why international negotiations over greenhouse gas emissions reach a stalemate. Per capita emissions in 1990 were only 0.489 metric tons in poor countries, but 3.426 in rich countries. Rich countries point to the unthinkable effects on the environment should poor countries follow the industrialization pattern of the rich countries, while poor countries point to the inequity inherent in freezing emissions at present levels, or demanding equal percentage reductions from all countries. Furthermore, every country will continue to use its forests to best commercial advantage and hope other countries will refrain from deforestation and provide carbon sequestration services to all. Since users get paid for timber they cut or cattle they raise after burning off tropical forests, but do not get paid for carbon dioxide sequestered, countries like Brazil, the Republic of Congo, and Indonesia, whose forests provide major sequestration services as "carbon sinks," have no incentive to preserve them. In sum, the free market has given us global warming and provides no incentives for anyone to do anything about it. And as long as globalization brings more decisions into the market nexus and increases pressures on countries to reduce environmental regulations to the lowest common denominator, globalization will aggravate global warming, just as it aggravates other forms of environmental degradation.

The last reason the present kind of globalization tends to abuse the environment is that market-driven decisions overvalue the present and undervalue the future.

- The profit criterion entails using the opportunity cost of investors' capital as the "rate of time discount" for comparing costs and returns in different periods. Yet this rate is far higher than can be justified for making decisions about how to use the environment. Since timing is a critical consideration in the efficient use of the natural environment, this leads to predictable short-sightedness

---

been much more severe over the past two hundred years. Currently, in the Washington, D.C., metropolitan area 28 acres of "green space" are lost *per day* to urban sprawl produced by "developers."

and overexploitation.

A reasonable case can be made for discounting future net economic benefits compared with present net economic benefits *if net national welfare per capita is growing.* If we interpret intergenerational equity as equal opportunity to enjoy economic well-being irrespective of generation, future well-being could be discounted by the expected rate of growth in per capita economic well-being. The idea is simple: if future generations are going to enjoy greater economic opportunities than we do, then the same amount of economic well-being delivered now should count for more than if it is delivered later.

But decision makers in the global capitalist economy are forced by competitive pressures to discount at a rate roughly equal to the normal rate of profit. And the normal rate of profit is significantly greater than the growth rate of Net National Welfare (NNW) per capita. When the value of "bads" such as pollution is subtracted from the value of all the "goods" produced, and when depreciation of produced and natural capital is taken into account, William Nordhaus and James Tobin estimate that from 1929 to 1965 the rate of growth of NNW per capita in the United States was only 1 percent per year. Herman Daly and John Cobb Jr. estimate that NNW per capita grew by only 0.8 percent from 1960 to 1970, and fell from 1970 to 1986, which means that average profit rates are surely several times higher than the growth rate of NNW per capita—and that whenever international businesses use those higher profit rates instead of the lower rate of growth of NNW per capita to discount the benefits the environment would provide later compared with the advantages of using the environment now, they opt to "use" the environment too quickly.

Corporate-Sponsored Globalization and Economic Democracy

The world's citizens did not vote for the kind of globalization that is going on. Instead, the process has been driven by business strategies and tactics for business ends, with governments abetting the process by incremental policy actions and by treaties that were often negotiated in secret. In the case of the North American Free Trade Agreement, NAFTA, and the European Monetary Union, EMU, publics were subjected to massive propaganda campaigns by the interested business media elites. Public opinion polls in the U.S. showed the general public against NAFTA even after incessant propaganda, but the mass media supported it, and it was passed. Polls showed persistent majorities in Europe opposed to the EMU as well, but a powerful elite successfully brought about the transformation.

Besides being the product of an undemocratic process, globalization weakens economic democracy in important ways. *First,* multinational corporations, or MNCs, have pushed for international agreements and IMF policies that encroach on the abilities of sovereign governments to adopt certain kinds of economic policies: Under NAFTA, governments are denied in advance the right to take on new functions. Any not asserted now are forever left to the private sector. In the Multilateral Agreement on Investment, or MAI, still under consideration, MNCs can fire people, abandon communities, damage the environment, and drive local companies out of business, while governments are prohibited from passing laws that infringe on their "rights" to do so. On the other hand, under NAFTA and to a greater extent under MAI, MNCs can sue governments, and disagreements are settled by unelected panels outside the control of democratic governments. International treaties and IMF policies also require governments to adopt certain kinds of policies whether they, or successor governments, would choose to or not. EMU conditions give primacy to budget constraints and inflation control. GATT, the WTO, and NAFTA all give top priority to corporate investor and intellectual property rights to which all other considerations must give way. IMF bailouts require governments to prioritize external debt repayment at the expense of economic development and social expenditures. Outlawed policies are invariably those that serve the interests of non-corporate constituencies, while policies required of governments are invariably consistent with the corporate agenda.

Second, global investors increasingly hold veto power over national economic policies. Social democratic policies are commonly interpreted as providing an unfavorable investment climate. MNCs and international finance increasingly respond to political parties and policies that serve ordinary citizens with threatened or actual exit. Spokespersons for the new global economy actually brag about the ability of capital to penalize "unsound" policies, and the fact that money capital now rules. Walter Wriston, former CEO of Citicorp, has repeatedly stressed that 200,000 financial market monitors in trading rooms control national monetary and fiscal policies "through a kind of global plebiscite"[1]—an intriguing conception of a plebiscite given that the number of people in the world is closer to 4 billion than 200,000! But Wriston is correct that the increasingly realistic threat of vetoes regularly causes social democrats to retreat to policies acceptable to global financial interests, leading social democratic political parties to accept and then rationalize neoliberalism in opposition to the preferences of the vast majority of their voting constituencies.

Third, according to pluralist theory, democracy rests on the existence of intermediate groups commonly referred to as "civil society." Over the past 200 years, labor unions have been arguably the most important organizations in civil society responsible for expressing the interests of an otherwise atomized and powerless population. The first way globalization erodes economic democracy is by weakening unions. One of the main objectives of MNCs abroad has been to tap cheaper labor sources. Labor is often cheapest and least prone to cause employer problems in authoritarian states that curb unions and enter into virtual joint venture arrangements with foreign capital, as in Suharto's Indonesia, the PRI's Mexico, and the CCP's China. Capital moves to such friendly investment climates in an arbitrage process that both encourages third world regimes to suppress their labor organizations and weakens labor in the advanced economies threatened by loss of jobs. As we saw above, globalization arbitrage also allows MNCs to pit governments against one another regarding which can run the most restrictive budgets and tightest monetary policies. Since these policies create unemployment, they indirectly weaken unions, civil society, and democracy as well.

Conclusion

Currently, globalization is both an active process of corporate expansion across borders and a structure of cross-border facilities and economic linkages. It is also an ideology whose function is to reduce any resistance to the process by making it seem both highly beneficial and unstoppable. While globalization may sometimes yield economic efficiency gains, the slowdown in the rate of growth of world GDP during the new neoliberal era, even before the onset of the global crisis in 1997, indicates that not even this is always the case. In every other respect, globalization is a major threat to progressive goals: equity, environmental protection, and democracy. Corporate-sponsored globalization should be recognized for what it is and fought at every level.

Notes

1. "Decline of Central Bankers," *New York Times*, September 20, 1992.

3

THE LATEST BUST
The Facts

By the fall of 1998 there was no need to listen to traditional doomsayers about the global economic crisis. The *Washington Post* began its front-page article covering the opening of the annual meetings of the International Monetary Fund and World Bank on October 5, 1998, saying:

> Forget about the Asian miracle, the Latin America revival, the Russian transformation, the mighty American economy and the triumph of free markets. The annual meeting this week of central bankers, finance ministers and private financiers at the IMF and World Bank is about holding the line and forestalling global economic disaster.

And in his speech to the assembled dignitaries, Paul Volcker, former chairman of the Federal Reserve Board, said: "Suddenly, it all seems in jeopardy. All that real growth—all the trillions in paper wealth creation—is at risk. What started as a blip on the radar screen in Thailand—about as far away from Washington or New York as you can get—has somehow turned into something of a financial contagion."[1]

Oxfam International offered the following assessment:

> The crisis now gripping East Asia bears comparison in terms of its destructive impact with the Great Depression of 1929. What started as a financial crisis has been allowed to develop into a full-fledged social and economic crisis, with devastating consequences for human development. Previously rising incomes have been reversed, and unemployment and under-employment has reached alarming levels. Rising food prices and falling social spending have further aggravated the social conditions of the poorest.[2]

As we saw in Chapter 1, the blush on the boom is seldom as bright as reported. But the human consequences of the bust are almost always far worse than revealed by the capitalist media. The view from Bangkok, Kuala Lumpur, Jakarta, Seoul, and Moscow is bleak beyond belief. Forget stock markets that in many cases lost well over half their value: The composite stock index fell 42 percent in Thailand, 74 percent in Malaysia, 80 percent in Indonesia, 29 percent in South Korea, and 86 percent in Russia—at the same time that stocks prices rose 31 percent in the U.S. and 54 percent in Germany. Forget currencies that depreciated dramatically: The Indonesian rupiah depreciated 73 percent, the South Korean won 33 percent, and the Thai baht 12 percent. Forget multibillion-dollar IMF bailouts that were in and back out of countries within weeks, leaving no discernible effect on economic prospects: In exchange for promises of fiscal austerity, price liberalization that doubles the prices of staples, and further reductions in restrictions on movements of foreign capital in or out of their countries, the IMF promised a $23 billion bailout for Indonesia, a $57 billion bailout for South Korea, a $17.2 billion bailout for Thailand, and most recently a $42 billion bailout for Brazil. Forget hundreds of billions of dollars of hard currency reserves that took decades to build up, wiped out in a matter of months. Forget the transfer of ownership of banks, factories, utilities, and natural resources—prized productive assets once valued in the tens of trillions of dollars—to foreign ownership at fire-sale prices. Forget all this because most of the people living in these East Asian tigers, suddenly turned water buffaloes with stripes, never owned stocks, resources, or foreign exchange in the first place.

What the lucky ordinary East Asians had gained from their economic "miracle" was a low-paying job in perhaps a modern factory, but more likely a dangerous sweatshop, instead of underemployment as a seasonal laborer or sharecropper in an unproductive agricultural sector. Only a tiny Asian elite gained substantial wealth from the flood of international capital into their countries. Instead of looking at currency values, foreign exchange reserves, and stock prices to gauge the human impact of the Asian crisis, we have to look at changes in employment, changes in output and therefore income, changes in real wages, changes in school enrollments, and changes in health statistics. Because, despite the fact that some of the Asian currencies and stock exchanges have recovered to some extent, there has been no recovery in production or employment to speak of almost two years after the financial crisis hit.

The eventual effect of the Asian crisis on output is still unknown since some of the economies are still shrinking and predictions of recovery have yet to be realized. But sometimes it doesn't take a weatherman to know which way the wind blows. In Thailand, where the crash hit earliest, GDP growth for calendar year 1997 was negative after being a positive 6 percent in 1996, while the World Bank estimates that GDP fell by 8 percent in 1998.[3] In Indonesia, where the crash came a little later, the growth rate for 1997 was only half the growth rate for 1996, and the World Bank estimates that GDP shrunk by 14 percent in 1998. In South Korea, the crash came late enough in 1997 to have little effect on growth in that year, but the World Bank estimates GDP shrank by 6 percent in 1998. The *Economist* estimated in early January 1999 that when the numbers are all in, GDP during 1998 would fall by 7.1 percent in Hong Kong, by 8.6 percent in Malaysia, and by 9.9 percent in Russia. Fixed investment is one indicator of the long-term effects of the crisis on output. The World Bank estimates fixed investment fell in 1998 by 28.7 percent in Thailand, 13.1 percent in Malaysia, and 43.5 percent in Indonesia. But estimating the eventual effects of the crisis on GDP is highly speculative since a great deal will depend on whether or not the crisis deepens in Japan or Brazil, or spreads to China, other countries in Latin America, Europe, or the U.S. And a great deal will depend as well on what measures different governments and international organizations do or do not adopt. We do know that during the first 12 months after the crisis hit, roughly 2,000 people lost their jobs each day in Thailand, where there were more than 2 million people out of work by November 1998, the unemployment rate had climbed from 2.1 to 7.3 percent, and, according to the World Bank, about 1 million had been pushed below the poverty line. In April 1999 the World Bank began its "country brief" on the Thai economy saying:

> The East Asian financial crisis has plunged the economy into a severe recession which has threatened to erode the gains of high growth rates over the past decade. In July 1997, the baht was floated, allowing it to plunge; production, investment, and domestic demand collapsed; and unemployment increased. The financial sector suffered from high levels of non-performing loans, corporate bankruptcies increased, and construction came to a standstill.

In its Update on Financial Sector Reform in Thailand, the World Bank reported that the Financial Restructuring Agency set up to take over the assets of the 56 finance companies that failed in the crisis had held three auctions, at the last of which 90 percent of the assets failed to receive even qualifying bids, and the 10 percent of assets sold did so at 37 percent of their face value. In the same update the World Bank reported that, according to the Bank of Thailand, non-performing loans at local commercial banks accounted for more than 46 percent of total loans as of October 1998.

In its country brief on Malaysia the World Bank informs us that for each 1 percent decline in GDP, the number of officially poor swells by roughly 50,000 people, which means 320,000 Malaysians descended to the ranks of the officially poor in 1998 according to World Bank estimates. In Indonesia 20 million people lost their jobs between September 1997 and September 1998 as the unemployment rate rose from 4.7 to 13.2 percent. Oxfam estimates that by the end of 1998 more than 100 million Indonesians were living below the poverty line—four times as many as in 1996. In South Korea there were 2 million newly unemployed by September 1998, and Paul Blustein reported in the *Washington Post* on April 17, 1999: "Korea's unemployment rate is 8.7 percent, the nation's highest in 33 years." Moreover, these unemployment figures do not reflect foreign "guest workers" who have been sent packing: 50,000 had already been sent home by South Korea, and 250,000 had been sent home by Thailand by September 1998.

In Indonesia UNICEF estimated that infant mortality would increase by 30 percent by the end of 1998. 250,000 clinics were closed down in less than a year for lack of medicines and volunteers who have left to scratch out a living for themselves and their families as best they can. The Indonesian minister of education estimated that 2.7 million children had dropped out of school in the first few months of the crisis. The Asian Development Bank estimated that more than 6.1 million had dropped out by September 1998. There is reason to fear that many of those school dropouts have gone to work in the $3.3 billion-per-year Indonesian child prostitution industry. Based on reports from its monitors in Indonesia, Oxfam International reported:

> In Yogyakarta, Central Java, where Oxfam works with street children, child prostitution is on the increase. Girls as young as ten are now turning to prostitution in a desperate attempt to feed themselves and their families. In the outer island of Flores, there has been a steep decline in visits to health centres because families cannot afford to meet fees. In West Timor several hospitals and health centres have shut down and basic antibiotics are now unaffordable. In Maluku, school attendance has declined by 60 percent.

In the Philippines financial contagion was largely prevented, but IMF-imposed austerity "medicine" is taking a terrible human toll. According to Oxfam, "fiscal discipline" included

> reducing the non-salary element of the health budget by one third. Allocations to preventative health care budgets for malaria and tuberculosis have fallen by 27 per cent and 36 percent respectively, and immunization programs by 26 percent. On the basis of data from the department of Health, Oxfam estimates that the reduced provisions for preventative health care programs will result in an additional 29,000 deaths from malaria and an increase of 90,000 in the number of untreated tuberculosis cases.

It is hard to believe things could get worse in Russia than they already were by the spring of 1998. But international default, large-scale bankruptcy, and the collapse of the rouble can only further reduce production, income, employment, and no doubt life expectancy. I let Stanley Fischer, Deputy Managing Director for the IMF, describe the scene as he tried to defend the actions of the IMF in Russia and point the finger of blame elsewhere. The following is quoted from a special report he prepared and presented to the IMF/World Bank–sponsored meetings in Washington, D.C., in October 1998:

> Ever since 1992 the IMF has been the world's main vehicle for assisting Russia and promoting economic reform. This was difficult from the start, for reformers never had full control over economic policy. Nevertheless, the world's stake in Russian reform was too critical not to make the effort. [Good old "noblesse oblige!"] Some progress was made ... but the extent of Russia's problem is hard to overestimate.... Since 1996 the Russian government has been in a race between its need to collect more taxes and a rising interest bill on its growing debt. In the second quarter falling oil and

commodity prices reduced export revenues, interest rates rose, and the government had to roll over $1 billion a week of GKOs, or short-term rouble-denominated debt. In July the international community faced a hard choice: whether to help Russia try to prevent devaluation. The adverse effects of a devaluation were clear and the reformist Kiriyenko government was making progress on taxes and in other areas. So the decision was made to help, recognizing that this was a calculated risk. An official package of $22 billion was assembled, on condition that the Russians undertake major tax reforms and a voluntary debt restructuring scheme for GKO holders to switch to longer-term dollar obligations was introduced. The take-up of this offer was, however, small. The program could still have been viable if GKO holders had been ready to roll over their maturing holdings. But after the Duma rejected two tax measures, and with doubts about the ability of the government to deliver on policy commitments growing, this did not happen. So the government was faced with an unenviable choice between devaluation, debt restructuring, or both. It chose both: the rouble was devalued, the GKO restructuring was imposed unilaterally and a temporary moratorium was put on private debt payments. The contagion following Russia's actions has been serious. The realization that Russia was, after all, not too big to fail shook investor confidence, although it is hard to believe that sophisticated investors who had earned an average of 50 percent a year on GKOs since 1994 really believed these investments were safe.

In other words, at this point Russia had abandoned further useless attempts to placate the IMF and the creditors it represents—the Russian government defaulted on payments to foreign bond holders and permitted the rouble to fall—and the IMF, in turn, had abandoned Russia—canceling further disbursements of the $22 billion bailout it had pledged. But the ultimate irony was still to come. In March 1998 IMF Managing Director Michel Camdessus returned to Russia to deliver a new IMF loan even though Russian officials had complied with none of the IMF's demands. The reason was quite simple: Russia was about to default on payments to the IMF itself! In order to preserve its perfect track record of never suffering a default on a loan, the IMF found itself in the embarrassing position of having to grant a new loan to a non-cooperating client sufficient to prevent default on its old one. As Paul Blustein explained in the *Washington Post* on March 31, 1999:

> Clinton Administration and IMF officials were at pains to demonstrate how, this time, they would avoid the pattern of throwing Russia good money after bad. The plan, they said, is for Moscow to get only enough international funds to ensure it can pay back the money it owes the IMF and World Bank this year—making the transaction a "bookkeeping operation," as some officials put it, in which the money would barely flow through Russian

hands before it was sent safely back to IMF headquarters in Washington.

In any case, Johannes Linn, World Bank vice president for Europe and Central Asia, told reporters in April the Bank projects "that real personal income in Russia will fall an average of 13 percent through 1999, with the extreme poverty rate rising to more than 18 percent of the population, while social expenditures by the government will fall by 15 percent." [4]

As I write in April 1999 the Asian flu has not spread to China. The jury is still out on whether Japan can jump-start its economy or is destined to sink deeper into recession.[5] The crisis in Latin America has been confined thus far to Brazil and Ecuador. Moreover, jitters in Europe and the U.S. remain only that so far, and have been largely confined to swings in the stock markets which have not yet affected the "real" side of the economy—i.e., production, income, and employment. Newspaper articles on the global financial crisis no longer appear on the front pages and have titles like "Global Financial Crisis Eases."[6] But the Institute of International Finance, which represents major private financial institutions investing in emerging markets, estimates that banks will withdraw $29 billion in 1999 compared with net withdrawals of $11.8 billion in 1998, and "direct investment flows—money invested in factories and machinery—will drop to a net $103 billion from $120 billion,"[7] which hardly sounds like the road to recovery. In any case, prognosticating is largely useless since much hinges on whether the current lull in the bust continues, or whether financial crisis breaks out anew and contagion spreads to other shores.

Notes

1. Quoted by Steven Mufson in "Economic Crisis Adds New Fears," *Washington Post,* October 5, 1998.

2. http://www.oxfam.org.uk/policy/papers/eabreif/eabrief2.htm.

3. Unless otherwise indicated, data are taken from country briefs and updates on the World Bank Web site (http://www.worldbank.org/data/countrydata.html), which provides more recent data than available in publications.

4. Robert Lyle, "World Bank: Hardship for Eastern Europe," April 29, 1999. Copyright 1999, RFE/RL, Inc.

5. If Japan does slip deeper into recession, it will be primarily because of lost export markets in the rest of Asia's collapsing economies, and because of its citizens' quite reasonable propensity to save when they have good reason to expect hard times ahead. It will *not* be because of some supposed "flaw" in the Japanese banking system, as is widely insinuated in Western circles. It takes real chutzpah for Western bankers who gave us the savings-and-loan crisis of the 1980s to wag their fingers at Japanese bankers who engineered the Japanese economic miracle of the 1950s, 1960s, 1970s, and 1980s.

6. Paul Blustein, *Washington Post*, April 26, 1999, A5.

7. Ibid.

4   UNDERSTANDING THE CRISIS
Helpful Tools

Understanding the inherent dangers of the credit system, the role of aggregate demand, the dilemmas of wealth-holding, and the relationship among exchange rates, interest rates, foreign exchange reserves, exports, and imports is crucial to sorting out the whys and wherefores of the global economic crisis of 1997–98.

Credit

If you barter your carrots for my potatoes, nothing that befalls me after our deal can affect you. You already have the potatoes you wanted for your stew in exchange for your carrots. If you sell your carrots for money, planning to use the money to buy potatoes from me, slippage between your stew bowl and your lip is conceivable. I may decide not to sell my potatoes after all. Or I may raise my price, or I may refuse to accept your money because I fear it may not be accepted by others—and I certainly can't put your money in *my* stew bowl. If you sell your carrots to me on credit, the possibilities for slippage increase. After eating your carrots I may fall ill and die. I may lose my job. I may owe other creditors who have prior claims on my ability to pay. In short, what befalls me after you sell me carrots on credit can affect you greatly if it affects my ability to repay you.

Of course, unless both borrower and lender expected to be better off as a result of a loan, no loan would ever be signed. For example, if you have excess seed corn and I have none, and if borrowing seed corn from you allows me to grow more corn than I could have otherwise, I can pay you back "interest," above and beyond your "principal," and still be better off than if I hadn't borrowed from you at all. In effect the loan allows me to be more productive, and the interest rate determines how much of this benefit I will keep and how much you will get. (Notice the loan allows *you* to benefit from the increase in *my* productivity, and even appropriate the lion's share of the benefit if the interest rate is high enough.) But if my crop fails, or if I get a lower price for it than either I or you expected, or if I use the proceeds to pay off prior creditors, I may be unable to pay you.

So monetized exchange is riskier than barter, and credit is riskier than monetized exchange—even without banks, future markets, options, buying on margin, derivatives, etc. How do these extensions of the credit relationship increase the risk that something may go awry, and the magnitude of the damage if something does? You deposit money into a bank account for safety, convenience, and the interest banks pay on deposits. The bank accepts your deposits so it can loan out your money at a higher rate of interest than it paid you. No doubt you knew this, but consider the implications. The bank did not simply introduce you, the lender, to a borrower, and then collect a fee when the two of you decided to consummate the loan—like the fee a matchmaker collects when a couple she introduces decide to marry. Instead, the bank weds you, the depositor, who have a legal right to withdraw any or all your money whenever you want. And then the bank turns around and weds the borrower, who is under no obligation to repay the principle, much less interest, until a specified date in the future.

But in this legal, financial bigamy the bank may be unable to fulfill his legal obligations to both wives. If the first wife insists on withdrawing more of her money than the bank kept in *reserve* after loaning to the second wife, who in turn spurns pleas for early repayment, the bank becomes *insolvent*. If the first wife presses her legal right and sues the bank for non-payment, a bankruptcy judge may declare the insolvent bank *bankrupt*, i.e., unable to meet its financial obligations. From the perspective of the depositor first wife, it is only her trust and patience that permits banking bigamy in the first place. From the perspective of the bigamist bank, it is only because depositor first wives refuse to make up their minds about whether they want to lend their money or use it themselves that there is any danger in bigamy. All flirtations with dangerous gender-laden humor aside, once one recognizes banking "bigamy" for what it is—a way to leverage one's own "capital" by using money that still belongs to *other* people to make *your* loans—the potential for problems comes as no surprise.

Futures markets, options, derivatives, buying on margin, hedge funds, and a host of other financial innovations all do one of two things: They either expand the list of things speculators can buy and sell and thereby speculate on, or they permit speculators to increase their leverage, i.e., use less of their own money and more credit, to buy something they hope to resell at a higher price. In other words, these, and any new "financial instruments" speculators dream up in the future, simply extend the credit system. If the extension provides funding for some productive activity that otherwise would not have taken place, it can be beneficial. But any extension—even those that do increase economic productivity—also increases the danger of the credit system by either increasing the number of things that might go wrong or by compounding the damage if the credit system comes crashing down. New "financial products" add new markets where bubbles can form and burst. Increased leverage compounds the damage from any bubble that does burst.

Nicholas Kristof provides a useful explanation of derivatives in his February 17, 1999, article in the *New York Times*:

> Originally called synthetic securities, derivatives are so named because they are derived from something else—an underlying stock or bond. They can be as simple as an option to buy a stock, or they can be complex products involving multiple currencies, loans and bonds. In effect they are re-

packaged securities, stuck together like a complex work of financial Legos. Their tremendous variety is reflected in the nicknames given to various kinds: the jellyroll; the iron butterfly; the condor; the knockout option; the total return swap; the Asian option.

But the key is that they are new financial commodities that increase leverage and expand opportunities for speculation:

> First, derivatives made it easier to make high-risk bets on Asia, but these were not publicly reported. As a result, no one had any idea how much betting was going on. "Derivatives enabled a lot of hot money to flow into Asia below the radar," said Frank Partnoy, a former derivative salesman and now an assistant professor of law and finance at the University of San Diego. Second, the riskiness creates a rush to cover bets when the market goes the wrong way, and this scramble sometimes causes wild market swings. As Mr. Partnoy explained the scramble: "It's as if you're in a theater, and say there are 100 people and you have the rush-to-the-exit problem. With derivatives, it's as if without your knowing it, there are another 500 people in the theater, and you can't see them at first. But then when the rush to the exit starts, suddenly they drop from the ceiling. This makes the panic greater." Third, derivatives increased the linkages from one country to the next. South Korea, in particular, invested in derivatives that were tied to Thailand, Russia, Indonesia and Latin America. So when those countries soured, South Korean financial institutions were badly hit as well. Derivatives allowed them high yields but also meant that they stood to lose far more than their principal.

The answer to the question of why derivatives flourished in Asia during the boom is simple, according to Kristof:

> The reason was that until the crisis, they were enormously profitable for everyone. Korean mutual funds managed to earn exceptionally high returns in part because of their derivative investment. Moreover, American banks often made huge sums selling these products in Asia. Jan A. Kregel, who has researched the issue as a senior fellow at the Jerome Levy Economics Institute in Annandale-on-Hudson, New York, concludes that in the boom years of both Thailand and Indonesia, Western banks made incomparably more money selling derivatives than making loans, and that in any case much of the lending was linked to derivatives as well. Most of the major American banks—Bankers Trust and Chase and J.P. Morgan and others— were actively selling derivatives in Asia.

There are two rules of behavior in any credit system, and both rules become more critical to follow the more extended, or leveraged, the system. Rule #1 is the rule all participants want all *other* participants to follow: DON'T PANIC! If everyone follows Rule #1 the likelihood of the credit system crashing is lessened. Rule #2 is the rule each participant must be careful to follow herself: PANIC FIRST! If something goes wrong, the first to collect her loan from a troubled debtor, the first to withdraw her deposits from a troubled bank, the first to sell her option or derivative in a market when a bubble bursts, the first to dump a currency when it is "under pressure" will lose the least, while those who are slow to panic will take the biggest baths. Once stated, the contradictory nature of the two logical rules for behavior in credit systems make clear the inherent danger in this powerful economic arrangement.

Aggregate Demand

John Maynard Keynes's greatest insight was that aggregate demand for goods and services is the "Leading Lady" in the capitalist "drama" concerning levels of production, income, and employment. If aggregate demand for goods and services is greater than current levels of production, the business sector has every incentive to increase production. If aggregate demand is less than production of goods and services, businesses have strong incentives to cut back on production. Capitalist economies do not necessarily produce as much as they are technically capable of producing. Instead, businesses produce what they have reason to believe they can sell, which is why aggregate demand—the sum total of household consumption demand, business investment demand, government spending, and foreign demand for exports—plays the leading role in determining how much will actually be produced, how much of the labor force will actually be employed (and unemployed), and whether or not demand will exceed supply for goods and services and thereby pull up prices, yielding inflation.

Higher levels of aggregate demand lead not only to higher production, higher income, and higher employment, but also to higher demand for labor, higher wages, and therefore lower rates of profit. They can also lead to higher rates of inflation, which tends to benefit debtors and hurt creditors. Lower levels of aggregate demand can dampen inflation, but can also reduce production and employment, depress wages, and redistribute income from debtors to creditors. Since government policies can influence aggregate demand, there are not only "general interests" but also "special interests" at stake in how and when they do so. The government can stimulate aggregate demand by increasing its own spending, by lowering taxes and thereby leaving more "disposable income" in the hands of consumers, or by increasing the money supply to drive interest rates down, thereby lowering the cost of credit and stimulating greater business investment and consumer spending on big-ticket items. Or the government can reduce its own spending, raise taxes, and tighten the money supply to reduce aggregate demand. Those who appeal to the government to reduce its own spending, and thereby aggregate demand, are usually careful to speak only of the general interest this might serve—combating inflation and reducing budget deficits. They do not bother to point out that anti-inflationary, budget-balancing policies also serve the special interests of employers vis-à-vis employees, and creditors vis-à-vis debtors. Similarly, many who recommend policies to boost aggregate demand point to the general interest of increasing production, income, and employment, but soft-pedal the special benefits for workers and debtors— presumably hoping not to provoke opposition from powerful financial interests who are also major political donors.

Holding Wealth

While most of us who live month to month don't have to worry about it, how to hold their wealth is the chief economic concern of the tiny minority who own most of the wealth. If they hold their wealth in dollars, it "earns" nothing and could be "eaten away" by inflation or depreciation of the dollar relative to other currencies. If they hold their wealth in stocks, they will get dividends but may suffer "capital losses" if stock prices fall. If they hold their wealth in bonds, they will get yields but may suffer capital losses if bond prices fall because interest rates in the economy rise above the yields their bonds pay. If they hold their wealth in foreign currencies, foreign stocks, or foreign bonds, they have similar worries. What a headache! There's just no foolproof way to "salt" wealth away and be secure that it will not erode—even if one were willing to forswear any interest in "earnings" from wealth. Even if one buys gold, diamonds, famous paintings, Persian rugs, or real estate, there is no guarantee that their market prices won't fall and wipe out a portion of one's wealth. And leveraging wealth to increase its "earnings" only increases the "downside" danger of serious capital losses.

These dilemmas lead to the following rules for those with significant wealth: Rule #1: Get your priorities straight. Remember that *how* to hold your wealth should be your major economic concern, and whether or not your government is helping you preserve your wealth or making it more difficult should be your first criterion for supporting or opposing any government. Rule #2: There is no such thing as "salting" wealth away. You must choose to hold your wealth in some particular form. Rule #3: There is no way to hold wealth that does not entail some risk that it will be lost. Even governments sometimes default on bonds, and even insuring wealth is useless if the insur*er* goes bankrupt. There are only more and less risky ways to hold your wealth. Financial advisors—people who advise other people how to hold their wealth—draw three conclusions from all this: (1) Don't put all your wealth eggs in one basket, i.e., diversify your portfolio. (2) Remember that the secret to wealth-holding is "knowing when to hold 'em and when to fold 'em," i.e., when to stay with one type of asset, and when to sell that asset and buy a different one. Moreover, the "when to hold 'em and when to fold 'em" decision should be guided by Rule #2 for proper behavior in credit systems: PANIC FIRST. And (3) the best "sucker play" is to find high-yield investments where someone *else* (foolishly) assumes the risk by agreeing to pay you if your investment goes bust. (As we will see, taxpayers are often the easiest "suckers" to bamboozle.)

In March 1999 Goldman Sachs, one of the last and certainly the most prestigious private partnerships on Wall Street, filed to sell a roughly 12 percent stake in itself to the public. In the process the firm explained to prospective buyers why the wealth-managing "industry" was a good industry to invest in. On page 8 of its 523-page IPO statement Goldman Sachs explains that during the 15 years from 1983 to 1998 while worldwide economic production tripled, the market value of equity stocks worldwide had soared sevenfold, and the amount of new borrowing worldwide had rocketed twentyfold! Can there be any doubt that highly leveraged wealth-holding activity is the tail that is wagging the dog of world production?

Foreign Currencies or Exchange

A currency is simply the "money" of a sovereign nation—the accepted means of exchange for goods and services in that country. It is accepted because the government says it is, or must be, accepted by those selling goods or services in that country. To get citizens to "accept" the national currency governments not only used to say they "stood behind" the currency, but pretended the currency was backed up and redeemable for gold, which the government pretended to have. Well, as you can imagine, governments easily succumbed to the temptation not to keep as much gold as currency they had issued, so this was never more than a confidence-inspiring, yet ultimately empty, publicity ploy. In any case, the world went off the "gold standard" long ago. (Charles DeGaulle could have told you that back in the late 1950s when, angered over U.S. international economic and foreign policy, he officially requested that the U.S. government redeem dollars the French government had accumulated for gold—only to be refused and chastised for being an ungrateful troublemaker by his former military superior, Dwight Eisenhower.) In any case, President Nixon brought official policy in line with reality in 1973 when he announced that the U.S. was going off the gold standard—i.e., the U.S. government was defaulting on any prior commitment to redeem its currency for gold.

So most countries have a national currency. "Convertible" currencies are simply currencies that can be bought and sold by anyone in international currency markets. The "price" any currency sells for is called its "exchange rate," or "value," and this price is usually quoted in terms of how many U.S. dollars a unit of that currency will buy. If a unit of a currency buys fewer dollars than yesterday, we say it has "depreciated" or "been devalued." If it buys more dollars, we say it has "appreciated" or "been revalued." The semantic difference is indicative of a change that took place a couple of decades ago in how international currency markets function. Today we operate under a system of "flexible" or "floating" exchange rates, which means that currencies appreciate or depreciate on a day-by-day basis according to fluctuations in supply and demand in international currency markets. We used to operate under a system of "fixed" exchange rates, in which each government would announce the exchange rate for its currency, but from time to time "announce" a new lower value, in which case we said the currency had "been devalued," or a new higher value, in which case we said the currency had "been revalued."

But the difference between fixed and flexible exchange rates is not as great as it first appears. Just as a business can "announce" a price for its product, governments could "announce" exchange rates for their currencies. But governments could no more dictate how many would want to buy or sell their currency at the "official exchange rate" than companies can dictate how many people will buy their product at the price they set. Governments inevitably faced the following dilemma under fixed exchange rates: If the demand for a currency was less than the supply at the official exchange rate, trading would start to take place at a lower rate in a "parallel" exchange market *unless* the government directed its central bank to enter the market and *buy* its own currency to eliminate the excess supply. If the demand was greater than the supply at the official rate, trading at higher rates would occur *unless* governments intervened by *selling* their own currency.

So the glue behind fixed-rate systems was the willingness and ability of central banks to intervene in the market for their currencies, buying or selling to eliminate excess supply or demand to preserve the official rate. Selling more of one's own currency to keep it from appreciating was never a problem, since a country can always print up more of its own currency. But intervening to buy one's own currency to avoid depreciation requires having stocks of other currencies (or gold) to buy *with*. Therefore governments were limited in their ability to support the value of their currency by the size of their "foreign exchange reserves," since once these run out, a government is powerless to eliminate any excess supply for its currency that might appear. On the other hand, the present system of flexible exchange rates is hardly one in which governments and central banks never intervene in the currency markets. As a matter of fact, central banks frequently intervene, using foreign exchange reserves to buy their own currencies to prevent depreciation, or selling their own currencies to prevent appreciation. Moreover, governments frequently negotiate agreements with one another, promising to help keep the values of their currencies within a specific "band." Governments "honor" these agreements by making the necessary interventions, buying and selling their currency when its exchange rate threatens to deviate from the band they had agreed to.

The relationship between exchange rates and exports and imports is as follows: If a country's currency depreciates, it takes less of foreigners' currency to buy the amount of the depreciated currency needed to buy exports from that country. In other words, when a country's currency depreciates, its exports become cheaper for foreigners to buy, so they will buy more. On the other hand, when a country's currency depreciates, it takes more of its currency to buy the amount of a foreign currency needed to buy imports from other countries. In other words, when a country's currency depreciates, imports become more expensive and consumption of imports will fall. Similarly, when a country's currency appreciates, demand for its exports decreases and its demand for imports rises.

The relationship between exports, imports, and employment is as follows: When the demand for exports rises, domestic production and employment will rise to meet the new demand. When the demand for exports falls, domestic production and employment will fall. When the demand for imports rises, production and employment will rise in foreign economies, not the domestic economy. When depreciation leads consumers to switch from imports to domestically produced goods, domestic production and employment increase. Currency appreciation leads consumers to switch from domestically produced goods to imports and thereby reduces domestic production and employment.

To understand the relation between interest rates and exchange rates, consider the following: Suppose interest rates in the U.S. rise relative to interest rates in Germany. The wealthy in both countries will now want to hold more of their wealth in U.S. bonds rather than German bonds to take advantage of the higher yields on U.S. bonds. To switch from German bonds to U.S. bonds, wealth-holders must sell the German bonds for German marks, use the German marks to buy dollars, and then use the dollars to buy U.S. bonds. This increases the supply of marks and the demand for dollars in the international currency markets, causing the mark to depreciate and the dollar to appreciate. As a result, any country that allows its interest rates to fall below rates in other countries risks depreciation of its currency. And any country whose interest rates rise above those in other countries can expect is currency to appreciate. In recent years the mobility of global wealth has increased substantially. Trillions of dollars of wealth can cross borders in days, and even hours, in response to changes in relative interest rates—thereby inducing large increases and decreases in the supply and demand for different currencies. Recent volatility of foreign exchange markets is largely a result of the size and mobility of "liquid" global wealth moving in response to changes or expectations of changes in relative interest rates. With these concepts we are now ready to explain how the Asian crisis started, why the IMF responded as it did, and why the results have been what they are.

5   HOW ASIA CAUGHT THE FLU
Analysis

With the help of the principles explained in Chapter 4 we are finally ready to answer the question posed in the introduction: How and why did the Asian crisis Walter Russell Mead described in his eyewitness account come about?

The Standard Explanations

First, let's dispense with the explanation for the Asian crisis that is preferred by those who orchestrated the great experiment in deregulation and globalization in the first place. People such as Goldman Sachs & Co. ex-CEO and Treasury Secretary Robert Rubin, Assistant Treasury Secretary Lawrence Summers, IMF Managing Director Michel Camdessus, IMF Deputy Managing Director Stanley Fischer, Federal Reserve Chair Alan Greenspan, and their politician mouthpieces like President Bill Clinton and British Prime Minister Tony Blair blame the Asian crisis on "crony capitalism," "lack of transparency," and policy failures of the governments of affected economies—rather than pointing the finger of blame at dangers built into the international credit system and policy failures of the IMF, the World Bank, and the U.S. Treasury Department and Federal Reserve Bank.

On November 10, 1998, Camdessus defended the IMF from what he termed "heavy criticism" in an op-ed piece in the *Washington Post*. Of course he was not referring to the "heavy criticism" that victims of IMF policy and the organizations that represent them, such as the 50 Years Is Enough Campaign, have voiced for decades. Objections from these sources—that IMF policy sacrifices the interests of poor, third world citizens to the interests of Wall Street by prioritizing debt repayment over economic development—were deemed to merit no response, and were always met by stony silence. However, Camdessus was sufficiently stung by criticisms from the likes of Henry Kissinger, Jeffrey Sachs, and Paul Krugman to finally lash back in public at detractors who must have seemed to Camdessus like rats deserting the IMF cruise ship, on which they had enjoyed free luxury berths for years, at the first sign of a leak. Camdessus defended the IMF from its new establishment critics as follows: "To my great surprise Kissinger actually suggested that the IMF 'too often compounds the political instability' and 'weakens the political structure' in countries it seeks to help by urging 'nearly invariable remedies' that 'mandate austerity' and include reforms that are too ambitious." Instead, Camdessus insisted that "the sources of the continuing Asian economic crisis originated in serious deficiencies in national economic policies." And "the very success of these economies made it especially difficult for political leaders in the region to accept the quiet counsel (yes, possibly too quiet!) of the IMF, the World Bank and other institutions to reform their financial systems and correct the glaring deficiencies of corporate governance." Instead of concluding that IMF policies had been wrong—besides perhaps speaking too softly while wielding their big stick!—Camdessus offered the following lesson:

> What Asian countries, Russia and too many other countries did *not* do was build sound financial systems quickly enough and give enough attention to the proper phasing and sequencing of capital account liberalization. Their "disorderly" liberalization now threatens to give liberalization itself an undeserved bad reputation. But orderly liberalization is the correct ultimate goal.

What do the great global liberalizers like Camdessus mean by "crony capitalism"? In plain English, they mean corruption and bribery combined with what they deem an unwise inclination on the part of governments to meddle with the market. While East Asian governments were no doubt as corrupt as most, what distinguished them was that their government agencies and central banks engaged in strategic planning in collaboration with businesses and banks to keep wages low and direct the flow of investment into industries well positioned to export to international markets. In other words, they "market-meddled" to implement the IMF-sponsored, export-led growth strategy! That is a lot more useful purpose to their "cronyism" than displayed by the "crony" U.S. Federal Reserve Bank when it helped orchestrate the bailout of the Long Term Capital Management hedge fund to protect the interests of some "crony" U.S. banks who stood to lose hundreds of billions if Long Term Capital went under.

By "lack of transparency," critics insinuate that the East Asian governments successfully concealed damning information about the state of their economies from international investors. But international investors were perfectly aware of the high debt-to-equity ratios of Asian banks and businesses to which they loaned. One could even argue that the higher interest rates in Asia compared with Europe and the U.S. at that time were solid evidence that investors recognized the risks they were taking. Moreover, it is a little far-fetched to argue after the fact that borrowers should be held responsible for failing to advertise any weaknesses in their situations to investors. Those who succeed in the international marketplace seldom do so by revealing their weaknesses to adversaries! Asian governments acted no differently in this regard than any government seeking to attract international investment ever has.

Moreover, it is hard to believe that Asian governments as corrupt as their critics claim would have proved difficult for wealthy international banks and investment houses, staffed by the brightest graduates from the top business schools in the United States and Europe, to bribe for any information they thought might be useful to them before risking hundreds of billions of dollars! Let's get real. If people want to talk of "lack of transparency" they should go back and look at deliciously devious, nationalistic third world governments in the 1970s, which enticed foreign investment in resource-extraction industries only to later nationalize foreign holdings in the name of protecting the national wealth. Or "dumb like a fox" third world governments in the early 1980s, which borrowed hundreds of billions only to discover to their surprise that their debt was "unpayable." The East Asian tigers were kittens—pliable and subservient to international capital—compared with these third world governments with claws. They were hardly the kind of governments to successfully play a wicked game of pulling the wool over the eyes of the international investment establishment—which, in a blatantly contradictory myth, is also portrayed as omniscient, far-sighted managers to be trusted with management of the world's productive resources.

But blaming the governments of economies that were victimized by the operation of international capital markets for failing to "give enough attention to the proper phasing and sequencing of capital account liberalization" is the most absurd claim of all. At every stage the IMF praised governments that liberalized rapidly and criticized governments that paid more "attention to proper phasing and sequencing." At every stage the IMF threatened cautious governments that they would lose out on the benefits of international investment as capital flowed instead to countries that liberalized more quickly and completely. And whenever the IMF gained leverage over any of these governments guilty of "disorderly liberalization," they compelled them to accede to even more hasty and ill-advised reforms. This line of argument is nothing more than a classic case of blaming the victim.

Not all members of the economic establishment have insisted on blaming the victims. But apparently retirement is conducive to honesty. In his luncheon address to the Overseas Development Council conference on "Making Globalization Work" on March 18, 1999, Paul Volcker, ex-chairman of the Federal Reserve Bank, said:

> My position is that the dramatic succession of international financial crises, and the adverse impact these crises have had on the economies of so many emerging nations, is a reflection of deep-seated systemic problems. I do not think the pervasiveness of these crises can be traced primarily to particular human or institutional failings either in the emerging world or the industrial world. Of course, there is no doubt such failings exist. They will continue to exist, despite our best efforts. But beyond these particulars, there are destabilizing forces at work, forces inherent in the organization (or lack of organization) of the international financial system in a world of free capital and money markets.[1]

In any case, if Michel Camdessus is interested in a better defense against the charge that misguided IMF policies permitted the crisis to evolve, and then aggravated the crisis once it appeared, he should plead that the IMF is largely powerless in the face of global capital markets that have outgrown their tamer—since there is some truth to this. But if the IMF pleads this defense on its own behalf, it would have to stop blaming the victims for the crises. For surely if the IMF is powerless to prevent the crises, then how much less powerful third world and "emerging market" governments must be to ride the tides of global capital sweeping in and out of their economies. But I suspect Camdessus is reluctant to cop a plausible plea because it leads to a guilty plea to a greater crime—the crime of having helped whip the swells of global capital to monsoon proportions, and having ordered the dismantling of restraining walls and dikes that provided precious little protection in the first place. What the IMF has most to answer for is the leading role it has played in liberalizing the international credit system whose dangers now frighten even those it was designed to serve.

What Actually Turned the Asian Boom into a Bust?

The truth is quite simple: International investment flooded into East Asia in the 1980s and 1990s because East Asia was a more profitable place to invest than anywhere else, and there was a sea of global wealth looking for dry land. Then, when investments financed by international capital became less profitable than all had come to expect, investors took flight, and chickens came home to roost in a highly leveraged global credit system.

The East Asian bust of 1997 and the Russian default of 1998 are hardly the first times mania followed by panic has struck an emerging market. In the 14th century an emerging market named England defaulted on international loans from banks in the Italian city state of Genoa. And in the 19th century the State of Mississippi defaulted on debts exactly as the Russian government just did. Finance has been international for hundreds of years, and globalization is nothing new. But as Nicholas Kristof and Edward Wyatt explain in their February 15, 1999, *New York Times* article titled "Who Went Under in the World's Sea of Cash?"

> Several forces have conspired in recent years to create a fundamentally new financial landscape that has fostered a world crisis. Money zips around the world faster than ever. In 1986 average global trading in currencies was less than $0.2 trillion. By 1998 this figure had risen to $1.5 trillion. [Meaning that currency trading increased at a rate of more than 55% per year between 1986 and 1998!] And deals are more reliant on borrowed money and can be riskier. In 1987 trading in financial derivatives was less than $1 trillion per year. By 1997 this figure had risen to $18 trillion per year. [Meaning trading in financial derivatives increased by more than 215% per year between 1987 and 1997!] By 1997 the value of derivatives traded during the year was more than 10 times the value of global

production during the year! The exposure of particularly European, but also Japanese and U.S. banks in emerging markets is equally astounding. In 1998 Europe had $656 billion in loans outstanding in emerging market economies, Japan had $211 billion, and U.S. banks had $120 billion.

This is an astounding story. If we want to know what has happened to the world economy at a glance, the answer is staring us in the face: International finance—liquid global wealth—has grown from a relatively sedate monkey on the back of the "real economy" of global production and consumption to become the proverbial 900-pound gorilla that sits ... wherever it wants. Not only that, the international finance gorilla is popping massive doses of "leverage uppers"! In large part, understanding the world economy has been reduced to understanding why a twitchy gorilla decides, from time to time, to change seats! In the words of Marc Faber, a prominent fund manager in Hong Kong, "It's no longer the real economy driving the financial markets, but the financial markets driving the real economy." [2]

Corporations in the U.S. and Europe enjoyed skyrocketing profit margins during the 1980s, but corporate strategy in the advanced economies was to downsize rather than invest rising profits at home. Japan was rolling in foreign exchange from decades of trade surpluses, making the yen queen of the currencies. In the late '80s it was the Japanese who led the pack in purchasing foreign stocks: Between 1985 and 1989 Japanese foreign stock purchases as a percentage of Japanese GDP rose from less than 60 percent to over 150 percent, which is an increase of more than 40 percent per year. With an appreciating yen it was cheap for Japanese corporations to buy the foreign currencies needed to buy or build subsidiaries in other Asian countries. In other words, direct foreign investment in Asia was cheap for Japan during the period. Besides, long-term Japanese strategy—labeled "crony capitalism" by some—called for transferring production of standard manufactured products to subsidiaries abroad to take advantage of cheaper foreign labor. In short, the Japanese—the biggest investors in East Asia—were busy rebuilding what they once called the "Japanese Asian Co-Prosperity Sphere."

During the 1990s, as the Japanese economy fell into the doldrums, the U.S. and Germany took over the leadership in purchases of foreign stocks. Between 1990 and 1998 U.S. foreign stock purchases as a percentage of U.S. GDP rose from 90 percent to 210 percent, which is an increase of 17 percent per year. Between 1990 and 1998 German foreign stock purchases as a percentage of German GDP rose from 50 percent to 250 percent, which is an increase of 50 percent per year. Of course not all these stock purchases were in emerging markets, and not all were in Asia. Predictably, Japan is more concentrated in Asian emerging markets, while Germany is more concentrated in Eastern Europe, and the U.S. is more concentrated in Latin America. But there was a dramatic redirection of international capital toward emerging markets. In 1991 the amount invested by mutual funds in emerging markets was less than $1 billion. By 1996 it was more than $32 billion, an average rate of increase of 620 percent per year! In 1980 less than 1 percent of pension fund assets in the U.S. were invested abroad. By 1997 that figure had risen to 17 percent. But more than pension funds, mutual funds, and other stock purchasers, international banks poured money into emerging markets, and East Asia in particular. In 1996, while international investors bought $50 billion worth of stocks and bonds in emerging markets, international banks poured in $76 billion.

And the biggest capital sponge was East Asia. In 1996, $93 billion poured into Indonesia, Malaysia, the Philippines, South Korea, and Thailand alone. In 1995, $77 billion poured into the same six countries. And in 1994 the figure was $41 billion. Between 1986 and 1996 Japanese private investment in Asia added industrial potential equivalent to that of three Frances! Neither Latin America, burdened by bad debt, nor stagnant African economies were attractive outlets for international capital during the late 1980s and early 1990s. The former "socialist" economies in East Europe and the former Soviet Union were tempting, but were not yet able to absorb large amounts of international capital quickly, and were much riskier in any case. The East Asian tigers were simply the best investment opportunities in the late 1980s and 1990s: disciplined work forces, low wages, pliable yet reliable governments, and no need to worry about inadequate internal markets to buy the goods produced in the early years because, the host governments agreed, the more goods destined for export the better. These were countries where, when the crisis hit, ordinary citizens carried gifts of family gold to Korean banks to help the banks meet foreign payments and thereby avoid "shaming" the nation. Truly a lender's dream!

But the storied Asian development model suffered from a problem known as the "fallacy of composition." When you are the first export-oriented economy, you are competing with high-cost Western producers. Your cheap workers, low taxes, and lax environmental laws allow you to underprice your competition and still make a bundle. But as more tigers joined the export-led growth circus, the circus wagons slowed under their weight. As the East Asian exporting economies competed more and more with each other rather than with Western producers, regional recession became more and more likely. The result? Investments that did not turn out to be as profitable as they were expected to be by both lender and borrower—a situation that leads to problems in any highly leveraged credit system—even if there had not been further complications.

But there *were* exacerbating complications: Many Asian banks borrowed dollars for "short" periods and loaned local currency for "long" periods. What does this mean? Asian banks borrowed dollars from international investors at high interest rates that fell due for repayment quickly. The banks used the dollars to buy local currency and make loans to Asian businesses at even higher interest rates, but these loans did not come due for longer periods of time. As long as new short-term dollar loans were available to the Asian banks, and as long as the Asian businesses were enjoying booming sales and high profit margins, the arrangement worked just fine for all concerned. International lenders got rapid turnover and high yields on their dollar investments. Asian banks earned high profits from a high volume of business conducted with a large spread between the interest rate they charged Asian businesses and the interest rate they paid international investors. And Asian businesses expanded their profit margins by leveraging their own financial investments with seemingly unlimited borrowed money. As long as the local currency remained reasonably stable vis-à-vis the dollar, which it would as long as export sales were strong, loans repaid in local currency could be converted to dollars and used to repay the dollar loans without any problem. Of course, this is just the happy coincidence of events that makes the lucky participants "thick as thieves," and that economics textbooks love to use to illustrate the benefits of credit systems. But what happens when something goes wrong?

When competition among tigers led to falling export sales, Asian businesses could not repay their high-interest loans from Asian banks. Moreover, falling export sales lowered international demand for the Asian currencies, leading to depreciation, which made dollars more expensive for Asian banks to buy. For both reasons Asian banks could not repay their short-run dollar debts in the usual manner—by selling local currency from repaid loans for dollars. Instead, Asian banks were forced to pay dollar-lender Peter by borrowing even more from some new dollar-lender Paul in the international capital markets. But this only helps if the underlying problem with Asian export businesses is short lived. If it persists, as it did, the stop-gap solution only aggravates the problem farther down the road. When the Asian banks finally couldn't meet payments on their dollar loans, it was too late. Their outstanding debt was too big and too short-term. As they scrambled to convert what local currency they had into dollars to meet their payment deadlines, they further depreciated the local currency.

When the international investors and currency speculators and local wealthy elites caught on to what was happening and obeyed Rule #2, PANIC FIRST, new dollar loans dried up overnight, and more local currency was dumped on the exchange market, causing further depreciation. While it is true that the devaluations *could* have made manufactured exports cheaper and more attractive to buyers, it was already too late to save the exporting companies. They were saddled with too much bad debt and couldn't get new credit from their local banks, which were also saddled with too much bad debt and couldn't get new credit from the international capital markets.

At this point there was no possibility of paying international investors Peter *and* Paul the dollars they were owed since the bottom had fallen out of the local currency, making the dollars necessary for repayment prohibitively expensive. Moreover, factories can't produce exports for sale if they can't afford to buy the imported inputs needed to make them. And this was certainly the case once the price of those inputs had been multiplied by depreciating local currencies. Asian factories, which fueled two decades of rapid growth, have not suddenly vanished. Their plant, machinery, management, and work forces are potentially every bit as productive as they were prior to July 1997. But now they are smothered in bad debts, which prevent them from getting working capital to start producing again. Whereas the credit system once allowed them to expand production and employment more quickly than they would have been able to otherwise, that same credit system now has them hamstrung.

In the Mexican crisis of 1994, the drop in the peso eventually stimulated demand for Mexican exports, which gave the Mexican economy a boost. But this could only happen because the Clinton Administration and U.S. banks with heavy investments in Mexico arranged to cordon off the bad debt from new debt, and provide sufficient new loans to allow Mexican businesses to start up again. But since *all* tiger currencies depreciated, and they compete mostly against one another, there is little boost in the demand for exports for any one of them from depreciation of its own currency. Moreover, on average, Asian businesses—particularly Indonesian businesses—import more of their machinery and materials for processing than was the case in Mexico, making the prohibitive increase in the price of imports caused by depreciation a bigger hurdle to overcome before the benefits of depreciation in export markets could be realized. Finally, once local currencies headed south in the Asian economies, local wealth fled into dollars and outside the country—eliminating the only other way to finance local business revival.

Were Asian bankers foolish to borrow hard currency for short terms and lend local currency for long terms? With the benefit of hindsight, of course they were. But they were no more foolish than international lenders who made massive unsecured dollar loans to Asian banks whose local loan practices they scarcely monitored. Were Asian governments foolish not to see the fallacy-of-composition problem in the export-led growth model? Of course they were. But they were no more foolish than the economists at the IMF and World Bank who scornfully dismissed previous development strategies and insisted that only export-led growth would be encouraged—failing to recognize that the success of the strategy hinged on only a few countries pursuing it. With hindsight it is easy enough to point the finger of blame at one group or another. But the underlying problem lay in the dangers lurking in the newly liberalized international credit system.

Notes

1. http://www.odc/program/volcker.htm.
2. Quoted by Nicholas Kristof and Edward Wyatt in "Who Went Under in the World's Sea of Cash," *New York Times,* February 15, 1999, A10.

6   THE IMF TO THE RESCUE

IMF-bashing, a popular sport on the left for years, has finally made it into mainstream culture. Unfortunately, some new mainstream players are now playing the sport at a higher level than many leftist veterans. Since Johnny-come-lately mainstream critics of the IMF do not share the left's progressive values and priorities, we can ill afford to let them beat us at our own game.

What Is the IMF?

Originally the IMF was a centerpiece of the Bretton Woods system of international regulation and control. But since 1980 the IMF has become the "point man" for efforts to deregulate the international economic system, and in particular remove restrictions on international capital flows. At the beginning of the 20th century anyone could move money across borders, which had long been the norm. But the Great Depression gave rise to a consensus that free international capital mobility too often results in capital rushing out of countries, sparking financial crises, and, therefore, that restrictions on international capital mobility were necessary. The Bretton Woods agreements and institutions, including the IMF, were designed to ensure that international currency markets would serve the interests of international trade rather than fall victim to disruptive financial speculation. As a result, during the Bretton Woods era, most countries, including the U.S., limited the rights of companies and citizens to buy foreign exchange or foreign securities or to invest overseas.

As memories of the Depression faded, financial managers and those whose wealth they managed successfully pressed for lifting restrictions. The tide shifted in Europe and the U.S. in the 1970s, and by the 1980s the U.S. government was actively pressing foreign governments to remove restrictions on the free flow of capital into and out of their countries. In 1985 President Reagan declared, "Our task is to knock down barriers to trade and foreign investment and the free movement of capital." Later, President Bush described his Enterprise for the Americas Initiative as a commitment to "free markets and to the free flow of capital, central to achieving economic growth and lasting prosperity."[1] The Clinton Administration, as it has on so many occasions since, took a reactionary Republican initiative with a well-heeled constituency it could ply for campaign contributions and pressed the pedal to the metal. Whereas Reagan and Bush had contented themselves principally with leaning on Japan, Clinton & Co. pressed for capital liberalization worldwide, especially putting the heat on smaller countries that were easier to threaten but also more vulnerable to international speculators once they had been disarmed. Clinton created the National Economic Council to wage the campaign, and invited Robert Rubin to be its first head. Jeffrey Garten, now a more pensive dean of the

Yale School of Management, but then a senior official in the commerce department and key member of the neoliberal "attack team," reminisced with Nicholas Kristof of the *New York Times* (February 16, 1999):

We pushed full steam ahead on all areas of liberalization, including financial. I never went on a trip when my brief didn't include either advice or congratulations on liberalization. We were convinced we were moving with the stream and that our job was to make the stream move faster. Wall Street was delighted that the broad trade agenda now included financial services. There wasn't a fiber in the bodies of Mr. Rubin, Mr. Kantor, and the late Commerce Secretary Ron Brown—or in mine—that didn't want to press as a matter of policy for more open markets wherever you could make it happen. In retrospect we overshot, and in retrospect there was a certain degree of arrogance.

Kristof goes on to point out that "the push for financial liberalization was directed at Asia in particular, largely because it was seen as a potential gold mine for American banks and brokerages," and to report that the biggest plum has just fallen off the tree Reagan, Bush, and Clinton have been shaking for almost two decades:

Japan is finally engaged in what it calls a "big bang" opening of its capital markets. The upshot is that American institutions are swarming into Tokyo and finally have a chance to manage a portion of the $10 trillion in Japanese personal savings. And when a big Japanese brokerage, Yamaichi Securities, collapsed 15 months ago, Merrill Lynch took over many of the branches—an acquisition that would have been unthinkable just a few years earlier.

In recent years the neoliberal brain trust in the Treasury Department has had little trouble convincing the neoliberal IMF leadership to play the role of "point man." Kristof reports:

In April 1997, Mr. Rubin headed a meeting in which finance ministers of the seven leading industrialized countries issued a statement "promoting freedom of capital flows" and urging that the IMF charter be amended so that it could lead the charge for capital account liberalization. Some Treasury officials now portray the effort to amend the charter as a fund initiative that they were not directly involved in, and indeed Britain was an early public backer of the idea. But a senior Treasury official acknowledges that the idea originated with American officials based in the fund who report to Treasury, and who consulted on the idea with members of the Administration. The records of the monetary fund—which was in many ways an instrument of American policy—also show that it was urging some countries in this direction already. In July 1996, the fund's executive board praised

Indonesia's "open capital account" and, a few months later, "welcomed the recent acceleration of capital account liberalization" in South Korea.

The IMF is traditionally thought of as the "manager" of the international credit system. But one could question whether the newly transformed international credit system *has* a manager. And one could debate whether "manager" would be an accurate label in any case. The IMF would have us believe it is more like a "social worker" for international "credit addicts." Polite IMF critics would use the word "policeman" rather than "manager" to describe the IMF's role. And angry critics see the IMF as nothing more than an "enforcer" or "rent-a-cop" in the employ of the international creditor syndicate: First, the IMF twists the arms of reluctant governments to remove restrictions on domestic businesses taking out international loans. Then the IMF comes back with the brass knuckles at collection time. I will simply present what the IMF does and analyze the predictable effects of its policies, leaving readers to choose their own label.

IMF Policy

The IMF has prescribed the same medicine for troubled third world economies for over two decades:

- *Monetary austerity.* Tighten up the money supply to increase internal interest rates to whatever heights needed to stabilize the value of the local currency.

- *Fiscal austerity.* Increase tax collections and reduce government spending dramatically.

- *Privatization.* Sell off public enterprises to the private sector.

- *Financial liberalization.* Remove restrictions on the inflow and outflow of international capital as well as restrictions on what foreign businesses and banks are allowed to buy, own, and operate.

Only when governments sign this "structural adjustment agreement" does the IMF agree to:

- Lend enough itself to prevent default on international loans that are about to come due and otherwise would be unpayable.

- Arrange a restructuring of the country's debt among private international lenders that includes a pledge of new loans.

Initial IMF policy in Thailand in the summer of 1997 is a good example not only of the policies imposed but of the international politics involved in arriving at IMF decisions. Nicholas Kristof provides the following account in his February 17, 1999, article in the *New York Times*:

> The Clinton Administration initially saw the Thai crisis as a replay of what
> had happened in Mexico in 1995, and prescribed the same mix of austerity
> and aid. So in the late summer of 1997, Treasury Secretary Robert E.
> Rubin and his deputy, Lawrence H. Summers, signed on to a standard Interna-
> tional Monetary Fund plan: spending cuts, high interest rates and a repair
> job on the Thai banking system.... The idea was that the sky-high interest
> rates would attract capital back to Thailand and stabilize exchange rates.
>
> But over the protests of the Fund the U.S. declined to contribute to a bail-
> out. Mr. Rubin and Mr. Summers were adamant that they could not con-
> tribute because of Congressionally imposed restrictions. The State and
> Defense Departments were unhappy with Treasury's tight-fistedness, but
> Treasury officials suggested sarcastically if any other department had a
> spare billion or two in its budget and wanted to help the Thais, it should
> feel free to do so.... Thailand appealed to Japan for financial help that
> summer of 1997, and officials in Tokyo say they thought seriously about
> arranging a big package of loans. But in the end they did not, partly be-
> cause Washington insisted that a rescue be made only through the mone-
> tary fund and only after imposing tough conditions on Thailand.... After
> initially bowing to Washington's desires and declining to rescue Thailand
> directly, Japan became more assertive as it saw the crisis worsen. In Sep-
> tember 1997, Japanese officials proposed a $100 billion bailout plan called
> the Asian Monetary Fund, to be paid for half by Japan and half by other
> Asian countries. This would not have cost the U.S. a penny, but Mr. Rubin
> was furious about it, partly because the Japanese had not consulted him....
> Mr. Rubin complained that the proposal would undercut American interests
> and influence in Asia, and that Japan would lend the money without insist-
> ing on tough economic reforms. Mr. Rubin and Mr. Summers succeeded in
> killing the plan, with the help of Europe and China. Many in Asia now re-
> gard that as a crucial missed chance, and there is real bitterness that the U.S.
> should have muscled in to prevent Japan's attempted rescue of its neighbors.

Since the alternative to signing an "IMF conditionality agreement" is *no* new
international loans—even to finance export sales and essential imports—combined
with threats of asset seizures abroad by international creditors; since there is no
longer a Soviet bloc that might decide to "scab" on an international creditor boycott and embrace a defaulting pariah to her bosom; and since an international lending boycott could bring most third world economies to their knees within months,
there have been few troubled countries in the past decade willing to stare down the
IMF and say "nyet" to its "devil's deal." If conditions continue to deteriorate we
may see more countries pushed to "just say no." In Chapter 9 we consider whether

this may be the best response and one progressives should encourage debtor governments to consider more seriously.

But until now the only countries able to put up any fight at all have been those that could play the "too big to fail" card. In the 1980s when Brazil owed more than $100 billion and Peru owed a little more than $10 billion, the saying in Latin America was: "If I owe you $10 billion, *I'm* in trouble. But if I owe you $100 billion, *you're* in trouble." In the Latin American debt crisis of the 1980s, the IMF backed down in face of Brazilian threats to default and agreed to a much more lenient program—effectively allowing the Brazilian economy to continue growing. On the other hand, when social democratic President Alan Garcia refused in 1985 to dedicate more than 10 percent of the value of Peruvian exports to debt repayment on grounds that paying more would make economic development impossible, the IMF excommunicated Peru from the international economic community. Peru was denied new loans even to finance exports, and the World Bank shut down not only its development projects but also its research projects in Peru, in solidarity with IMF policy. The greater the "exposure" of international creditors—and in particular U.S. creditors—the better the deal debtor countries have been able to extract from the IMF and the creditors it represents, because the larger the debt, the more negative the consequences of default *for the entire club of international creditors* as well as for the country that defaults.

But what are the consequences of standard IMF policy? The predictable consequences for most residents of the troubled economy—who are *not* the ones who took out the international loans—have always been disastrous. Tight monetary policy and skyrocketing interest rates not only stop productive investment in its tracks, stampeding savings into short-run financial investment instead of long-term productive investment, they prevent many businesses from getting the kind of month-to-month loans needed to continue even ordinary operations. All of which leads to more unemployment and a fall in production and therefore income. Fiscal austerity—raising taxes and reducing government spending—further depresses aggregate demand, also leading to reductions in output and increases in unemployment. To the extent that government programs had been improving people's lives, reductions eliminate those benefits. Privatization of public utilities, transport, and banks is always accompanied by layoffs. Whether productivity and efficiency are improved in the long run depends on how badly the public enterprises were run in the first place, *and* whether private operation proves to be an improvement. One of the most glaring inefficiencies of "structural adjustment" even on its own terms has been that in its haste to reduce public-sector budgets, the IMF has seldom taken the time to try to distinguish between poorly run and well-run public enterprises. In its crusade to privatize, the IMF routinely lumps efficient public enterprises together with "white elephants" that provide poor service to the public while paying bloated salaries to relatives and political supporters of ruling political parties. The IMF ignores the possibility that the private enterprise replacement could be even worse. But irrespective of whether the long-run effects of privatization are positive or negative, in the short run it adds to unemployment, depresses demand, and aggravates recessionary pressures.

In the short run, hasty removal of restrictions on international capital flows makes it easier for wealthy citizens and international investors to get their wealth out of the country, i.e., removing "capital controls" facilitates capital flight, further reducing productive investment, production, income, and employment. In the long run, removing capital controls further exposes the local economy to the vicissitudes of global capital mobility, including the disease of "contagion" (discussed below). No wonder IMF conditionality agreements are also known as "austerity programs." They not only depress productive investment and thereby sacrifice economic development; they depress aggregate demand and increase the gap between actual production and the meager productive potential that exists in troubled economies.

Surprisingly, there is little disagreement about the above effects. If you did not reveal that some part of the package was part of an IMF structural adjustment program, most trained economists would predict the above consequences for each part taken separately. What *is* controversial is the IMF claim that in the long run these policies will rebound to the benefit of the local economy and its inhabitants. That prediction is based on the assumption that once the economy has gone through the pain necessary to right its sunken ship in the sea of international credit, the benefits of "orderly liberalization"—revived exports and new international investments, and the increased productivity they supposedly bring—will trickle down to everyone. Fortunately for those who defend IMF policies, those benefits are only predicted to materialize in the future, so whenever someone points out that they have yet to show up, the IMF and its apologists can always answer that the trickle is still working its way down.[*]

---

[*] While the World Bank has been surprisingly outspoken in criticisms of IMF austerity policies since the advent of the Asian crisis, and has hastened to finance social safety nets in affected economies, one cannot help but see some "good cop, bad cop" element in IMF/WB teamwork. In its October 1998 report on Indonesia, Oxfam International stated that "one of its central concerns is the discrepancy between the macro-economic policy framework of the IMF, and the social policy framework of the World Bank. In effect, these are pulling in different directions. The World Bank is in the hapless position of erecting social safety nets, which are collapsing under the weight of rising poverty and mass unemployment resulting from IMF programs."

But IMF policy is not designed to help the majority in troubled economies. It is intended to help international creditors in the short run, and increase returns on global capital in the long run. The truth is that any benefits to residents of local economies are only an afterthought. How are IMF policies supposed to solve the short- and long-run problems of international creditors and global capital? In the short run creditors want to be repaid by their third world borrowers. They want to be repaid on schedule, they want to be paid the high returns they were promised when the loans were made, and of course they want to be repaid in dollars. Their chances of getting repaid are better the higher the value of the local currency of their borrowers, since profits in that currency must be turned into dollars to repay them. Their chances of being repaid are better the larger the surplus of exports over imports, since that is one source of dollars to repay them. The only other source of dollars is new international loans or reductions in the repatriation of earnings of current international investors. But new loans mean further risk and exposure. And restrictions on international capital outflows are the last thing creditors anxious to get their money back are likely to support! So anything that props up exchange rates or boosts exports and lowers imports is in the interest of international creditors.

How do high interest rates and depressed economies—which is what IMF policies create—prop up currencies and generate trade surpluses? High local interest rates attract international capital in the short run, which increases demand for local currency and boosts its value. Lower levels of production mean lower incomes, lower demand for imports, larger trade surpluses, and therefore also upward pressure on the value of the local currency. Expanding the trade surplus and propping up the local currency are the only ways local debtors can pay off their international creditors quickly, and *that* is why they are the key to every component of IMF stabilization policy. Preserving the value of local currencies is talked of as if it were a major boon to the troubled economies. But in fact the deflationary monetary and fiscal policies used to stabilize the currency and reduce imports bring a halt to productive investment, growth, and development, and throw the local economy into a recession or worse, with dramatic drops in production, income, and employment. But the disastrous effects on the local economy are irrelevant to those who impose the policy, because protecting the local currency and expanding the trade surplus are necessary if international creditors are to be repaid.

But when the IMF intervenes in a crisis, monetary and fiscal austerity is not sufficient to pay all the creditors back—particularly the ones whose loans are coming due immediately. That is where the second part of the IMF agreement comes in. The IMF loans the debtor country enough money to pay off what it calculates will be the unpayable portion of the outstanding loans coming due. In other words, they provide a "tide over" loan to avoid defaults, which will supposedly be repaid once the beneficial effects of the austerity measures—that is, the effects beneficial to creditors—kick in. This bailout of international investors whose loans have become unpayable is designed to spare them losses from their "risky" investments and also to prevent panic that defaults might trigger from spreading to other parts of the international credit system. The IMF also tries to convince private investors to make new loans as well, since this reduces the amount the IMF has to come up with. The easiest private investors to convince, of course, are the very ones who made the loans that are in danger of not being repaid. Essentially the IMF threatens them that if they do not participate in the debt-restructuring plan and cough up new loans, the IMF will abandon the salvage operation and they will go unpaid. But a sizable commitment of IMF money is necessary to convince these lenders that the waters will now be safe for new loans and they will not be throwing good money after bad.

But where did the IMF get the money to loan $17.2 billion to Thailand, $23 billion to Indonesia, $22 billion to Russia, $57 billion to South Korea, and $41.5 billion to Brazil? After all, the IMF is not an international central bank, like the central banks of sovereign nations, which truly are "lenders of last resort" for their national banking systems because they do have an unlimited capacity to make new loans in their national currencies. The answer is, the IMF gets its budget from "assessments" of member governments—like the $18 billion supplemental assessment the Clinton Administration lobbied Congress to approve in light of the Asian crisis, which well-heeled Republicans, after months of populist bluster on Capital Hill, finally signed off on in the last-minute budget deal before the 1998 election recess. In other words, the IMF budget comes from the taxpayers of member nations and any interest the IMF receives from loaning those taxpayers' money.

Notice the not-so-subtle shift in risk-bearing buried in IMF rescue packages. International investors make loans and collect high yields in part because there is risk of default. But when danger of actual default rears its ugly head, the IMF makes the loans necessary to avoid default, at which point the creditors are paid back in full, after having enjoyed the high yields. But if the IMF can always be counted on to ride to the rescue, it turns out there is no risk for the international investors! Does this mean the risk simply disappears? Hardly. First of all, even when the IMF rides to the rescue, there is no guarantee the cavalry will arrive in time with enough fire power. Russia *did* default despite IMF attempts to shield the international credit system from such a shock. But even when an IMF intervention prevents default on loans coming due immediately, there is still a risk that despite the best efforts of the IMF to turn the troubled economy into a debt-repayment machine, it may still fail to pay off all it owes further down the line—including all it now owes to the IMF—which is exactly what has occurred in Russia in 1999. So the IMF arranges a full payoff for the original investors—including interest payments enlarged by riskiness—and then assumes the risk of default itself. We have re-found the risk, but who is the IMF that now bears the risk? Suddenly the IMF is the taxpayers of its member countries who pay assessments. Of course, if the IMF loans eventually get repaid, then member-country taxpayers who made the loans through the IMF will also be repaid, and one can argue—as the IMF and its supporters certainly do!—that the IMF bailout never actually ended up costing the taxpayers a penny. But that is hardly the point. If the IMF loans themselves are not repaid, the taxpayer has paid off the international lenders by assuming their risk and getting stiffed in their stead. But even in cases where the IMF loans are repaid, taxpayers of member countries subsidize international lenders who receive a risk-inflated rate of return, when in fact it is the taxpayers who end up assuming the risk.

So IMF bailouts are not bailouts of debtor countries and their economies at all. That's just a popular misconception that some find convenient to let pass uncorrected. IMF bailouts are bailouts of international investors because that is who gets the money. It is the great sucker play of the wealthy in the late 20th century, where international lenders enjoy the high yields while taxpayers assume the risk. Of course, in broad terms it is just one more case of privatizing the benefits of an economic activity—in this case, international lending—and socializing the burdens associated with that activity: risk of international default. Through IMF bailouts taxpayers of member nations provide underwriting services to international investors, for no fee, and provide insurance for international investors, for no fee. A sweet deal when you can get it.

The windfall for international banks in the bailout of South Korea was atypical only in its extreme one-sidedness and its sheer magnitude. As Kristof recounts (*New York Times,* February 17, 1999):

> By Thanksgiving Day 1997, it was clear to all top officials in Washington that South Korea was on the brink of an economic catastrophe. After five hours of conference calls among top American officials, President Clinton telephoned President Kim Young Sam of South Korea and told him he had no choice but to accept an international bailout. Mr. Kim bowed to the inevitable and accepted a bailout that swelled to $57 billion, the biggest ever. But with that money now flowing into South Korea, Western banks saw a chance to take it and run. The banks called in their loans, hoping to flee while they could. Mr. Rubin quietly called the heads of major banks and urged them to reschedule their loans, and in the end they did. But the bailout still ended up bolstering Western banks. South Koreans lost their businesses and in some cases were even driven to suicide. But foreign banks—among them Citibank, J.P. Morgan, Chase Manhattan, BankAmerica, and Bankers Trust—were rewarded with sharply higher interest rates (two

to three percentage points higher than the London interbank rate) and a government guarantee that passed the risk of default from their shareholders to Korean taxpayers.

In the words of none other than Nobel laureate and dean of conservative economists Milton Friedman: "IMF bailouts are hurting the countries they are lending to, and benefitting the foreigners who lent to them. The United States does give foreign aid. But this is a different kind of foreign aid. It only goes through countries like Thailand to Bankers Trust."

In the long run wealthy international investors and multinational businesses want to be able to invest anywhere they choose, at the highest possible rates of return, with the lowest possible risk of losses. If foreign stock markets look profitable, they want to be able to invest in them without restrictions, and they want to be able to get out whenever they wish. If public utilities or state-owned industries look profitable, they want to be able to buy them. If agriculture or real estate looks profitable, they want to be able to buy land in foreign countries. Whenever rising wages, business taxes, or environmental laws raise the costs of doing business in one country, they want the threat of moving to be as credible and frightening to local governments and populations as possible. That means they want to be able to go into and out of business anywhere, anytime. Like owners of professional sports franchises in the U.S. who play the citizens and governments of a city and state against each other in bidding wars to subsidize franchises with new stadiums and accompanying infrastructure at taxpayers' expense, international capital wants to be able to play the workers and governments of all countries against one another, collecting promises of low wages and exemptions from taxes and environmental regulations, to keep the long-run returns on international capital as high as possible. Privatization, particularly at fire-sale prices, and elimination of restrictions on international capital flows and ownership permit international investors to buy up the most attractive assets in economies that fall under IMF management and permit them to get their profits out of the country whenever they like. That is why the IMF insists on conditions to liberalize capital flows and foreign ownership as well as fiscal and monetary austerity when it has a country over the barrel of pending default.

Anyway, that's how IMF policies were *supposed* to work. And for the most part that's how they did work prior to the onset of the Asian crisis. So what went wrong? Why is George Soros, who made tens of billions from international investments in the 1980s and 1990s, suddenly saying things like: "International financial authorities are inadequate. The methods they used were inappropriate and unsuccessful in arresting the spread of the collapse. I'm not against the IMF but I think it should change its policies." [2] We can be sure it is not for the same reason others joined the 50 Years Is Enough Campaign long ago.

IMF Failures in Asia and Russia

So the question here is not why IMF policy has failed to lead to economic recovery and development in troubled economies. It was never designed to do that and, in fact, explicitly sacrifices investment, growth, and development of troubled economies at the altar of debt repayment. The question is why standard IMF policies suddenly failed to serve the interests of international investors who had loaned to East Asia and Russia—and why it is possible that the exact same policies and the $41.5 billion loan to Brazil may also prove ineffective.

The IMF cure for Southeast Asia's creditors was too little, too late and suffered from the same problem as the Asian development strategy—the fallacy of composition. Depressing the Thai economy helps Thailand's creditors get repaid—assuming the baht can be stabilized and world aggregate demand holds steady. Depressing the Malaysian economy helps Malaysia's international creditors get their money back—assuming the ringgit can be stabilized and world demand holds steady. Depressing the Indonesian economy helps Indonesia's creditors get repaid—assuming the rupiah can be stabilized and world demand holds steady. Depressing the South Korean economy can help Korea's creditors get repaid—assuming the won can be stabilized and world demand holds steady. But that is a lot of assuming.

The first problem was that the IMF interventions failed to stabilize the local currencies. Instead of reversing devaluations, IMF interventions triggered capital flight and thereby aggravated depreciation of local currencies. Instead of reassuring international investors that they would be repaid, announcements of IMF agreements—pledges of billions of dollars of IMF loans to repay loans coming due and promises from local governments to forgo growth and development in order to be able to better repay their creditors—were interpreted by international investors as a sign that problems were even more serious than they had previously realized. The appearance of the fireman did not calm guests in the house on fire; it sounded the alarm announcing to all that Rule #1—DON'T PANIC—had already been broken. So of course everyone implemented Rule #2—PANIC FIRST!—and headed for the exits. As you read in the evaluations of Stanley Fischer (in Chapter 3) and Michel Camdessus (in Chapter 5), the IMF would have us believe that "the market"—meaning international investors—did not find pledges of reform by troubled governments convincing. For Fischer the problem was the Russian Duma. International investors did not believe Russia would actually collect more taxes or relax capital restrictions. For Camdessus the problem was that Indonesian and Korean promises to end crony capitalism were not credible. The more obvious explanation is that international investors did not find the IMF credible! They doubted that the size of the IMF bailout was going to prove sufficient to reverse the outflow of capital given the magnitude and mobility of international capital. This wasn't Mexico in 1994, where overexposed U.S. banks and the U.S. government had every reason to do whatever was necessary to keep Mexico from going down the tubes—especially if they could get the U.S. taxpayer to assume the risk of guaranteeing the loans necessary for the bailout. International investors decided the Asian tiger economies were *not* too big, or too important, to fail—and they were right. Besides, the international investors didn't have to stay in the house and run the risk that the fireman would fail to put out the fire. They could PANIC FIRST—dumping local currencies and withholding new loans—and wait to see what happened. If the fire got put out, they could always go back in later, buying local currencies and assets at lower prices than when they dumped them, and making new loans when business conditions had actually picked up.

The second problem was that once the Thai, Malaysian, Indonesian, and Korean economies fell into recession, the assumption that world aggregate demand would hold steady was no longer valid. Just as the booming Asian economies had provided the boost in aggregate demand that sustained world economic growth in the early 1990s, depression in this region now threatens to pull the rest of the world's economies down with it. Stagnant Japan faces lost export sales to depressed Asian economies. China may devalue the yuan if Asian tiger currencies do not recover, to prevent loss of Chinese export sales to Asian competitors—in which case Japan, the U.S., and Europe would lose export sales to China. Belatedly, the danger of a world recession or worse—due to falling aggregate demand—became apparent even to IMF leaders, who backpedaled on their insistence that the troubled Asian economies implement fiscal and monetary austerity at their meetings in Washington in early October 1998.

Now that it is apparent that IMF policies may not even solve the short-run problems of international creditors, it is natural to ask where all this might lead. The great fear of those who have yet to suffer the effects of the global crisis is summed up in the word "contagion."

Contagion

When people speak of "contagion" they mean that problems in some part of the world economy might spread to other parts of the world economy. Since the world economy is more highly integrated than ever before, this is almost a tautology. But exactly what kinds of contagion must we fear?

One kind of contagion is that falling output and incomes in a major region of the world economy depress the demand for exports from other regions, which can tip stagnant economies into recession. Just as recessions within a national economy have dangerous self-reinforcing dynamics that are harder to counter once they start to build, the same is true for the world economy. So one transmission mechanism for contagion is that any significant decrease in aggregate demand for goods and services can lead to further decreases in aggregate demand that spread to sectors not initially affected. This is the problem of self-aggravating, rather than self-correcting, recessionary dynamics that Keynes finally explained to the "academy" during the 1930s, and that is certainly one concern today.

Will recession in a group of Asian tigers spread to Japan because their demand for Japanese exports has dropped dramatically? Will the stagnant Japanese economy stifle recovery in the crippled East Asian economies that find it harder and harder to sell exports to Japan? The Japanese government finally succumbed to international pressure to try to pull the Japanese economy out of recession through expansionary fiscal and monetary policy. As reported in the *Washington Post* (November 16, 1998):

> Prime Minister Keizo Obuchi today unveiled public spending and tax cut plans worth $196 billion as the embattled government struggles to stop Japan's economic slide. The economic plan includes $49 billion in income and corporate tax cuts, and $147 billion in spending projects. Those projects include public works spending of $66.5 billion and vouchers to encourage consumer spending. The government plans to spend $8 billion with a goal of creating 1 million new jobs and, in particular, to promote the employment of middle-aged and elderly people. Japan's banking crisis has made it difficult for companies to get bank loans. The package includes $48 billion to combat this credit crunch, by extending the scope of loans and loan guarantees by government banks such as the Japan Development Bank.

But analysts are by no means confident that the package will prove sufficient. In an article published October 27, 1998, John Pomfret of the *Washington Post* worried:

> Can China hold out? Surrounded on all sides by economic crisis, China's government has shifted into economic overdrive—going on a risky multi-billion-dollar spending spree. In an effort to save jobs, it has loosened credit standards to pump funds into moribund state-owned industries. A growing China could help ease Asia out of its economic doldrums. But stagnation could force the devaluation of the yuan [to stimulate demand for Chinese exports, which are beginning to lose foreign markets to Southeast Asian countries whose currencies have fallen], which could in turn trigger another round of competitive devaluations around Asia and deepen recession throughout the world.

Will depression in Russia, where GDP is now less than half of what it was in 1991, spread to Germany and Europe? Whether or not the new IMF rescue plan for Brazil—which is identical to its rescue plans for Thailand, Indonesia, and

South Korea—succeeds in preventing devaluation and default, it will surely create a serious recession or worse. Will a Brazilian recession drag Argentina, Uruguay, and other South American economies down with it? Would adding a recession in Japan, China, or Brazil to the depressions already raging in the Asian tigers and Russia be a sufficient blow to U.S. exports to trigger a recession here? These are all worrisome possibilities of "aggregate demand contagion."

But when analysts talk of contagion they usually mean a different kind of problem. Once investors take fright of one Asian tiger or one emerging market, they may decide that all investments in what were once called "undeveloped economies" but are now referred to as "emerging markets" are riskier than they had previously believed and pull out of economies that are perfectly sound. To distinguish it from the contagion of falling aggregate demand we can call this "psychological contagion." In case it was not already apparent, international investors are not omniscient. They make assessments based on partial information—not primarily due to lack of transparency, but because guessing is the nature of investment! In any case, they have no choice but to make assumptions and to generalize. But being somewhat self-aware, they constantly revise their expectations. So if their assessment that the Malaysian ringgit is sound is based, in part, on their assessment that the Thai baht is sound, when they discover that the baht is not, indeed, as sound as they had believed, they logically revise their estimate of the reliability of the ringgit. If international investors' estimate of the reliability of Russian government bonds proves wrong, why would they not downgrade their evaluation of government bonds in other emerging markets? Some talk as if downgrading estimates of Belarus government bonds without looking any further into Belarus is illogical. But when you discover, to your surprise, that Yeltsin has defaulted on some Russian government bonds and announced a 90-day moratorium on foreign-debt repayment, do you wait until the 90 days are up to discover that Russian banks are only able to pay $2 billion of the $6 billion due on forward currency contracts to foreign banks before pulling out of forward currency contracts on the Belarussian as well as the Russian rouble, and before getting out of Belarussian as well as Russian government bonds? What would be illogical would be *not* to downgrade Belarussian bonds and currency based on new Russian evidence pending an investigation of Belarus.

When Russia defaulted, the contagion spread to Brazil as well, but for a slightly different reason. Hedge funds that had greatly leveraged their purchase of Russian bonds, and international investment banks that had invested in those hedge funds, found themselves in desperate need to sell other assets they owned to meet payments on their Russian bond losses. Brazilian currency, bonds, and stocks happened to be the most sensible assets to sell in their portfolios. In the end, the result was the same—a sell-off of Brazilian debt that triggered a much larger sell-off as other investors, who had not been burned by the Russian default, applied Rule #2: PANIC FIRST.

Some would have us believe that psychological contagion is a kind of illogical and primitive reaction and, as more intelligent and rational international investors out-compete those who move with the herd, the problem of contagion will recede. They would have us believe that new international accounting procedures and disclosure rules will fundamentally change the business of international finance. Then sound Latin American currencies will not be unfairly punished by investor flight to hard currencies stimulated by depreciation of Asian currencies that truly were not sound. Then reliable governments in emerging markets will not be punished by investor flight to U.S. treasury bonds when an irresponsible Russian government defaults on its bonds. Unfortunately, contagion is quite logical, and there is no reason to expect that a more liberalized global credit system will prove less prone to mistaken generalizations, because the problem goes much deeper. The problem is that people are making important economic decisions with precious little information and knowledge. We have permitted the world to be turned into a place where a handful of people in a handful of cities—many less than 10 years out of MBA programs, who are now managers of currency, bond, and securities departments of international banks, insurance companies, and investment funds—are the ones who decide what will be produced, how it will be produced, and how it will be used everywhere on the planet. Worse still, they do not even make these decisions consciously; they make them as a by-product of their guesses about how profitable and risky different investment opportunities are in different world financial markets. The heirs of Adam Smith try to lull us to sleep, crooning: "Markets make the best decisions." But no market has ever made a decision—for good or bad. Those with power to act in markets make more and more decisions when more and more decisions are relegated to the marketplace. One can criticize the lack of democracy when so few make the economic decisions that affect so many in today's world economy. One can criticize the inequities of how those decisions distribute the burdens and benefits of world economic activity. And since those making the decisions are at the very top of the world's pyramid of wealth or are in their employ, there is every reason to worry about the implications for economic justice. We should all continue to criticize the functioning of the global marketplace as anti-democratic and inequitable. But at this point it is not only lack of democracy and equity that are at issue: Simple lack of competency has become apparent to any willing to see. Psychological contagion is the consequence of the incompetency inherent in the new world economic system that the liberalizers and deregulators have given birth to.

Finally, besides aggregate demand contagion and psychological contagion, there is contagion spreading from the financial sector to the real sector. This can happen in two ways. Since we have wedded investment and production to the credit system, a collapse of the credit system will lead to a collapse of investment and production. Since we have wedded consumption to income and wealth, a decrease in either will lead to a decrease in consumption, which could, in turn, lead to a fall in production. As we saw in Chapter 1, the collapse of the credit system in Thailand, Malaysia, Indonesia, and South Korea has led to steep drops in investment and production that have already erased much of whatever economic progress was made in the previous 15 years. The effects of the collapse of the Russian credit system in August 1998 further depressed production, and the conditions imposed on Brazil in exchange for the IMF bailout have reduced output dramatically there as well. Or, contagion can spread from the financial sector to the real sector through the "wealth effect." Syndicated columnist Robert Samuelson worried in an op-ed piece in the December 30, 1998, *Washington Post*:

> At least two aspects of the boom cannot last forever. One is the huge surge in stock prices, which are up 28% in 1998, as measured by the Standard & Poor's Index of 500 stocks. This follows gains of 34% in 1995, 20% in 1996, and 31% in 1997. The second thing that cannot continue indefinitely is the national shopping spree. The consumer savings rate is usually 4% to 6% of disposable income; in 1998, it was almost zero. Ominously, these two trends are connected. Americans are spending so much in part because they feel so wealthy. Economist Bruce Steinberg of Merrill Lynch notes that higher stocks have "added roughly $8 trillion to household net worth during the past six years." (Net worth is what people own minus what they owe.) In turn, strong consumer spending shields production and profits from the baleful effects of foreign recessions. This props up stock prices. So there's a mutually reinforcing confidence game. High stock prices boost consumer spending; and strong consumer spending boosts stocks. If either falters, the other may follow suit.

There is no doubt the spectacular rise in the U.S. stock market has stimulated consumption demand in the U.S. in the past few years. If the U.S. stock market suffers a significant drop, the consumption of wealthy U.S. households will decline significantly as well. Since a drop in any part of aggregate demand can lead to further decreases in aggregate demand, this could trigger a recession or aggravate recessionary dynamics that began elsewhere. And any number of things could burst the bubble on Wall Street. Price-to-earnings ratios are over 30 to 1—record levels that would usually portend a correction. According to First Call, an advisory service, in early 1998 stock analysts expected operating profits for the S&P 500 companies to rise 14 percent. They have risen only 2.6 percent. As Mark Weisbrot explained in "Neoliberalism Comes Unglued" (Z magazine, September 1998), the U.S. stock market is significantly overvalued, and a hefty "correction" is likely at some point even if there are no contagion effects from other stock markets. But drops in other stock markets around the world could spread to the U.S. stock market if investors conclude that stocks in general are not a safe way to hold their wealth. And "corrections" are by no means always marginal. The Japanese stock market in 1989 was almost three times its present level. In any case, a shift by U.S. wealth-holders from stocks to bonds would lead to a large drop in the U.S. stock market and certainly create powerful recessionary dynamics in the real economy here in the U.S. I see no reason to disagree with Samuelson's outlook for the U.S. economy in 1999:

> What now sustains confidence is confidence. The economy has done well; so people expect it to do well. Perhaps it will. Unemployment is low, inflation is trivial. People expect interest rates to drop further. But few of the threats of 1998 have vanished. Japan's economy is still shrinking; Latin American economies are still weakening; the U.S. trade deficit is still growing; global overcapacity in many industries is still expanding. These trends imperil jobs and profits: the props of confidence. The shopping spree could end; stocks could drop; a recession could ensue.

Notes

1. Quoted by Nicholas Kristof and David Sanger, *New York Times,* February 16, 1999, A10.

2. Quoted by Reuters from a speech given in Sofia, Bulgaria, published in the *Vancouver Sun,* November 10, 1998, as "Global Crisis Needs New Solutions, Soros Says."

7　　WHAT SHOULD WE WANT?
WHAT SHOULD WE FEAR?

> Our task is not to make societies safe for globalization, but to make the
> global system safe for decent societies.
>
> —John Sweeney, President, AFL-CIO,
> Davos, Switzerland, January 2, 1999

Most of us want to produce and consume. We want to save in case of emergencies and for our retirement. We want to work with more and better tools and equipment. Right now we are forced to pursue these goals in an economic system that ties these activities to a credit system. We are told the credit system helps us produce, consume, save, and invest more efficiently. We are never told there may be better ways to organize our economic activities—ways that are equally or even more productive and efficient, ways that allow people to control their own economic destinies and cooperate with one another more equitably. And we are seldom told that along with the supposed benefits of wedding production, consumption, saving, and investment to the credit system, there are increased dangers. The dangers become apparent only after a crisis has interrupted our economic lives. We are also seldom told that once production, consumption, saving, and investment are governed by the credit system, those few with substantial wealth will be primarily interested in preserving and expanding their wealth through speculation in the credit system. Nor are we warned that, if given their heads, the wealthy will do everything in their power to increase their opportunities to speculate and to increase their leverage when they do speculate. We are unlikely to be told this not only because we might hesitate to consent, but also because few of the wealthy even recognize themselves as speculators in the credit system. But that is, indeed, what they are. They do not work, they do not produce; they trade money for stocks, stocks for bonds, dollars for yen, etc. They speculate that some way to hold their wealth will be safer and more remunerative than some other way. Broadly speaking, the global credit system has been changed dramatically over the past two decades in ways that pleased the speculators. As long as the effects on the rest of us were incremental losses of economic democracy and justice, or as long as those affected severely were the poor and the powerless, in the poorest and least powerful parts of the global economy, attempts to organize people to oppose the changes faced the usual problems of apathy, inertia, and lack of resources. But now that the increased dangers of the liberalized global credit system have become more apparent, the opportunity for a "general reconsideration" is improved. First, we must become more aware of the dangers that are clearly apparent. Then, we must distinguish between changes that would benefit only the speculators—some of whom are also having second thoughts about how well some recent changes have served their interests—and changes that will make the lives of the rest of us more productive and safe, as well as more equitable and democratic.

What Should We Want?

If international trade and investment *actually* reduce global inequality, if they *actually* reduce strain on the environment, if they *actually* increase global economic democracy, and if they *actually* improve global efficiency, we should be all for them. The problem, of course, is that international liberalization and neoliberal policies have *actually* accomplished just the opposite. They have increased international inequality and environmental destruction, decreased economic democracy, and probably decreased global efficiency as well. The irony—and, therefore, the tease—is that international trade and investment *could* be helpful in all the above ways. After all, it does not *have* to be a bad thing for advanced economies to make capital and technical know-how available to less developed economies, and for all countries to produce what they produce best. But instead of living up to their potential, international trade and investment have been, shall we say, "classic underachievers" that show no signs of mending their wayward ways.

- *Global efficiency* is increased if we citizens of the world produce goods and services that are more valuable to us with less strain on ourselves and on the environment.

Hopefully when defined in this way—as it should be—it is clear why improving global efficiency is desirable. "Efficiency" has earned a bad reputation among progressives only because: (1) it is often elevated above other desirable goals, like economic equity and democracy, which we are urged to sacrifice for its sake, (2) it is often erroneously equated with "profitability," which is logically distinct, and often at odds with, efficiency in practice, (3) it is often forgotten that more leisure and more pleasant work environments are also "goods" that may be more valuable than the consumer goods we produce through their diminution, and (4) those who use the word often fail to account for environmental degradation when they calculate and speak of efficiency.

- *Equity* means matching economic benefits to economic sacrifices.

If, and only if, someone makes greater sacrifices in carrying out their economic duties do they deserve greater economic benefits commensurate with their greater sacrifices. This definition of equity holds for people from different countries once we join each other in a global economy, just as it holds for different citizens of the same country and national economy. But it is pointless to require that international economic policies instantaneously eliminate any and all international inequities, since there is no policy that could wipe out the historical legacy of international economic injustice in one fell swoop (just as there is no policy that can immediately eliminate all inefficiencies in the world economy). Instead, what we should insist on is that reforms and policies *reduce global inequities*. Since there is no credible evidence that those living and working today in less developed countries (LDCs) are making fewer personal sacrifices than those living and working today in more developed countries (MDCs), the requirement that programs and policies reduce global *inequities* reduces to the requirement that they reduce global *inequalities* in income—which is something we know well enough how to measure.

- *Economic democracy* means having decision-making input to the degree one is affected by an economic decision.

This conception of economic democracy incorporates those aspects of economic "sovereignty" that are legitimate: the citizens of a country are overwhelmingly the most affected by decisions about what their country produces, consumes, and invests. But "decision-making input in proportion to the degree affected" also recognizes the legitimacy of a degree of international participation in economic decisions that, for example, affect the amount of global warming or cross-border acid rain others must put up with. Again, there is no point in insisting on perfection before giving our approval to a policy, since no policy can achieve global economic democracy overnight. But there is every reason to insist that any changes in the global economic system move us closer to achieving economic democracy as defined above.

- Finally, besides economic efficiency, equity, and democracy, it makes sense to ask that changes in the global economy promote greater respect for *diversity* and *solidarity* between peoples of different countries rather than more resentment and enmity—since the consequences of the latter are all too clear.

So if more equity, democracy, efficiency, solidarity, and diversity are what we want from international economic reforms, what are the basic changes required to achieve them?

What Is Needed?

First, we need to "get prices right." This may sound terribly mainstream, and by "first" I mean "logically first," not "getting prices right should be our first priority." But the fact is, without more accurate estimates of true social opportunity costs it is impossible to know how to redeploy productive resources internationally to achieve efficiency gains. And to ignore the problem that current market prices are in many cases very poor indicators of true opportunity costs is behaving like the ostrich that, when confronted with a difficult situation, sticks its head in the sand. Almost nobody worries about this, and almost none of the reforms being discussed even in the most progressive circles address this problem. The reason is simple. You can't address this problem without admitting a fundamental flaw in the market system, and you can't fix the problem without resorting to non-market methods to correct for a host of daunting externalities that include, but go far beyond, major environmental effects of producing, transporting, and consuming different goods and services. This means that until such time as markets are replaced by a different social procedure that more accurately estimates the true social costs of providing goods and services, and does not leave major consequences uncounted and "external" to the economic decision-making process, we need an international institute that commissions non-market surveys and studies to estimate the magnitude of the most significant external effects in the world economy. Only then can we correct market prices before estimating opportunity costs in different countries, calculating comparative advantages, and making decisions about more efficient patterns of international specialization and trade.

The *second* thing that cannot be left to the free market is the terms of trade and international interest rates, because if we do leave this to the free market, global inequality will only continue to increase. Again, discussion, negotiation, and conscious cooperation among international trading partners and lenders and borrowers must replace market interactions. Something like the New International Economic Order proposed by representatives of the Non-Aligned Movement in the 1970s, but ignored and then rejected by the OECD countries, the IMF, the World Bank, and all the regional development banks, is required if pursuit of efficiency gains from international trade and investment is not to lead to growing international inequality. As I discuss in Chapter 9, improving international labor and environmental rights and standards, while worthwhile, will not solve this problem. So it is a strategic mistake for progressives to allow the issue of international equity to be reduced entirely to the issue of international labor and environmental rights and standards. Terms of trade must be set politically to distribute more than half of the efficiency gains from international specialization to LDCs and less than half to MDCs.

Third, not only must the terms of trade be set so as to award poorer, not richer, countries most of the benefits; all international lending must pass a simple equity test: The poorer a borrowing country, the lower interest rates it should receive from international lenders. Obviously, market forces tend to do just the opposite, as past success is the best "collateral" guaranteeing future success. I am not suggesting interest rates on loans to poorer countries that leave lenders worse off than if they did not lend at all. I am merely pointing out that for international lending to alleviate global inequality, interest rates must be set to award more of the efficiency gain from lending to the borrowing country the poorer the borrowing country is.

Fourth, we must solve the problem of lost production due to credit bubbles and crises that lead to massive unemployment of productive resources. Whether it is possible to redesign the international credit system so that it serves the purpose of facilitating productive investment rather than affording greater opportunities for speculation, and how best to do so, is the subject of most of the ongoing debate I evaluate in Chapter 8. But that discussion cannot even sensibly begin until the problem of old debt that has much of the world's productive capacity currently tied up in knots is solved. It is no longer only the cause of international equity that begs for debt forgiveness. Restarting production in Africa, Asia, Latin America, and Russia requires massive debt forgiveness, as does eliminating future dangers to the credit system already visible on the horizon.

What Should We Fear?

- There is every reason to fear that another credit crisis could appear overnight in any of a dozen countries, and that the financial "contagion" might spread wider and deeper than it has previously.

The recently liberalized international credit system is seriously out of control. The volume of speculative transactions associated with wealth-holding motives now dwarfs the volume of transactions associated with production, consumption, and investment. Global wealth managers are a constant threat to the normal functioning of smaller economies by parlaying any signs of economic strength into unstable speculative bubbles, and by overreacting to inevitable weaknesses and thereby creating unwarranted panics. When successful international speculators like George Soros tell us "international financial authorities are inadequate" and world-renowned financial regulators like Paul Volcker warn of "deep-seated systemic problems" in the international financial system, only an ostrich would bury its head in the sand. Moreover, global capital is increasingly able to veto any government policies of which it disapproves. Business threats to move jobs elsewhere should wages, business taxes, and labor and environmental standards not be to their liking are increasingly credible. In other words, globally mobile business capital has started an accelerating "race to the bottom" in workers' living standards. And globally mobile financial capital is increasingly able to veto national fiscal and monetary policies it finds inconvenient.

- There is every reason to fear that depressed conditions in one region might spread to others.

The continuing depression in East Asia could further depress Japan. The Japanese recession could reduce Japanese imports enough to trigger a recession in China. A string of competitive devaluations between China and the wounded East Asian tigers could push the entire region into deeper depression. The depression in Russia and further defaults on European loans could further depress the German economy, and thereby the rest of Europe. The depression unfolding in Brazil could easily spread to Argentina and the other Mercosur economies, or if the financial crisis in Brazil flares again, Venezuela or Mexico could join Ecuador on the casualty list from Brazilian contagion. If a significant part of Latin America falls into recession, U.S. exports to the region could drop by enough to start a U.S. recession—the last bastion of economic denial. Or, a long-awaited "correction" in the U.S. stock market, which is certainly more overvalued than the Japanese stock market was 10 years ago before it dropped by 30 percent, could depress consumer spending enough to trigger a recession that even Chairman Greenspan would find hard to stop with monetary manipulations to reduce interest rates by a percentage point or two. Any of these scenarios remain distinctly possible over the next 12 months.

Not only are the risks of aggregate demand deflation very high at present; many governments are handicapped by crippled banking systems, or political and ideological obstacles, from pursuing corrective measures should the need arise. Governments in Japan, China, and all the depressed East Asian economies find it difficult to stimulate production by easing credit because so many of their banks are overloaded with bad debt. A host of political complications make it difficult for the new European Economic Union to agree on an orderly path of expansion. And the ideology of fiscal conservatism has reached hegemonic proportions in large parts of the Western electorate, posing serious obstacles to quick fiscal expansion even when that policy is obviously called for. Moreover, international coordination of macroeconomic policies has not been this dysfunctional since the Great Depression, and there is no lender of last resort on the horizon for the only credit system that any longer matters—the global credit system. But these dangers do not compare to something else that is already happening.

- Our greatest concern should be something little discussed among Western economists, politicians, and pundits who are wont to worry about almost any other aspects of the global economy except the fact that Western multinational corporations and banks are busy buying up the most attractive economic assets the third world has to offer at bargain-basement prices.

At their present pace they may undo, in only a couple of years, all progress toward reclaiming their economies made by anti-imperialist third world movements and governments over the past 50 years. They may do it without the cost of occupying armies. They may do it without firing a shot. Just as the painfully slow reduction of inequality and wealth within the advanced economies won by tremendous organizing efforts and personal sacrifices of millions of progressive activists during the first three quarters of the 20th century was literally wiped out in the past 20 years, all the gains of the great anti-imperialist movements of the 20th century may soon be wiped out by the policies of neoliberalism and its ensuing global crisis. This should be our greatest fear, and this must be what we most resolutely condemn and do everything in our power to stop.

What may become the greatest global "asset swindle" of all time works like this: International investors lose confidence in a third world economy, dumping its currency, bonds, and stocks. At the insistence of the IMF, the central bank in the third world country tightens the money supply to boost domestic interest rates to prevent further capital outflows in an unsuccessful attempt to protect the currency. Even healthy domestic companies can no longer obtain or afford loans, so they join the ranks of bankrupted domestic businesses available for purchase. As a precondition for receiving the IMF bailout the government abolishes any remaining restrictions on foreign ownership of corporations, banks, and land. With a depreciated local currency and a long list of bankrupt local businesses, the economy is ready for the acquisition experts from Western multinational corporations and banks who come to the fire sale with a thick wad of almighty dollars in their pockets. In an article published in the *Washington Post* on November 28, 1998, Sandra Sugawara described how this process is unfolding in the first Asian domino to fall, Thailand:

> Hordes of foreign investors are flowing back into Thailand, boosting room rates at top Bangkok hotels despite the recession. Foreign investors have gone on a $6.7 billion shopping spree this year, snapping up bargain-basement steel mills, securities companies, supermarket chains and other assets. "Thai companies have been in distress longer, so maybe they are further along the road in getting beyond the denial stage," said an American acquisitions expert. "They are at the stage where they are thinking it's better to sell assets now than in six months, when they will be worth less." In many other countries, distressed companies still are holding out for better deals.
>
> The reluctance of Thai banks to make loans is a predicament found throughout Asia these days. During the boom years of the early to mid-1990s, Asian banks lent money aggressively, sometimes recklessly. When the recession hit, many of those loans went bad. In Thailand, more than one-third of the loans may not be repaid. Short of capital, banks are holding on tight to the money they have, making it hard for even healthy companies to expand. The decision of the Thai government and Thai banks not to prop up Thai companies also has accelerated the restructuring process

and helped foreigners close deals. For example, Charoen Pokphand, one of Thailand's largest business groups, sold its Lotus discount store chain to Britain's Tesco PLC and its share of a motorcycle plant and brewery in Shanghai to pay off creditors and protect its core agribusiness.

A few pages behind stories about layoffs and bankruptcies are large help-wanted ads run by multinational companies. General Electric Capital Corp., which increased its stake in Thailand this year through three major investments in financing and credit card companies, is seeking hundreds of experts in finance and accounting, according to one ad. Another said that Bank of Asia, acquired this year by the Dutch bank ABN Amro, is hiring in many job categories, including credit analysts and risk managers.

All this is in an article that Sugawara's editor at the *Washington Post* ironically chose to title "Thai Economy Shows Signs of Rebounding"! Nicholas Kristof expanded on this theme in the *New York Times* on February 1, 1998, in an article titled "Asia's Doors Now Wide Open to American Business":

> Many experts believe that one of the most far-reaching consequences of the Asian financial crisis will be a greatly expanded American business presence in Asia—particularly in markets like banking that have historically been sensitive and often closed. "This is a crisis, but it is also a tremendous opportunity for the U.S.," said Muthiah Alagappa, a Malaysian scholar at the East-West Center in Honolulu. "This strengthens the position of American companies in Asia." Market pressures—principally desperation for cash—and some arm-twisting by the U.S. and the IMF mean that Western companies are gaining entry to previously closed Asian markets. And the timing, from the U.S. point of view, is perfect: regulations are being eased just as Asian banks, securities, even airlines are coming on the market at bargain prices.... Stock prices and currencies have now plunged so far that it may cost less than one-fifth last summer's prices to buy an Indonesian or Thai company. "This is the best time to buy," said Divyang Shah, an economist in Singapore for IDEA, a financial consulting company. "It's like a fire sale."

According to a recent study by the Stern business school in New York, the top 10 investment banks almost doubled their share of fee-based and advisory business in the global capital markets since 1990.[1]

> "Most of these countries are going to go through a deep and dark tunnel," said Jeffrey Garten, dean of the Yale School of Management. "But on the other end there is going to be a significantly different Asia, and it will be an Asia in which American firms have achieved much deeper penetration, much greater access. You would have seen a lot of this anyway over the

next decade or so," Garten added. "But it's going to happen at an order of magnitude and with a degree of speed that nobody could have conceived of just six months ago."

If this forthright admission of the imperial consequences of the Asian crisis is not enough, Kristof goes on to explain:

Among the most important beneficiaries as Asian markets open are the American financial service companies, especially those like Citibank that have already been building their presence in Asia. Opportunities are also expected for industrial companies like General Motors or large retailers like Walmart that operate in sectors where barriers to entry have been common. Asian countries have been steadily opening their economies in recent years, but they have generally been much more willing to admit McDonald's than Citibank. Governments in the region have sometimes owned banks and almost always controlled them, and leaders frequently regarded pinstriped American bankers as uncontrollable, untrustworthy and unpredictable barbarians at their gates. And now the gates are giving way. A clear indication that the Asian crisis would further the American agenda came in December, when 102 nations agreed to open their financial markets to foreign companies beginning in 1999. It is unclear how the pact will be carried out, but it marks an important victory for the U.S., which excels in banking, insurance, and securities. Fundamentally, that agreement and other changes are coming about because Asian countries, their economies gasping, are now less single-minded in their concern about maintaining control. Desperate for cash, they are less able to pick and choose, less able to withstand American or monetary fund demands that they open up.

In every Asian country in crisis, the same story is unfolding, as Kristof makes clear:

In Thailand, under pressure from the monetary fund, the government was forced to scrap a regulation that limited foreign corporations to a 25 percent stake in Thai financial companies. Citibank has signed a memorandum of understanding on the purchase of a major Thai bank, First Bangkok City Bank. Thai government officials have predicted that foreign companies will soon dominate Thailand's financial sector.

In Indonesia, the government has said foreign banks can take a stake in a major new bank that will be formed from several weaker ones. The national car project is also losing key benefits, which effectively opens up the auto market to greater foreign competition. "All our stocks and companies are dirt-cheap," said Jusuf Wanandi, the head of a research institute in Jakarta, Indonesia. "There may be a tendency for foreigners to take over everything."

Almost two weeks ago Hong Kong, already the most open market in Asia, resolved an 18-month domestic negotiation by announcing the end of a local company's monopoly on long-distance telephone service. The result will be virtually complete liberalization of the territory's telecommunications market.

As for Japan, it agreed on Friday to a landmark package, resisted for many years, to liberalize air travel links to the United States. The aviation agreement will mean more opportunities for American airlines. In the financial arena, Merrill Lynch is talking about buying part of the branch network of Yamaichi Securities, a giant Japanese firm that collapsed in November. In December, Fidelity Investments opened counters in Japanese banks to sell mutual funds directly to Japanese customers, and foreign companies succeeded last year in doubling the amount of Japanese money that they manage, to a total of more than $20 billion. One consequence ... is the "big bang" opening of Japan's financial markets, beginning April 1.... The big bang is expected to create new opportunities for American and European banks and security firms. "I'm worried that the American banks will come in and take over everything after the big bang," said a Japanese banker.

The *Washington Post* reported on March 27, 1999:

Renault SA of France signed a $5.4 billion agreement today to become the largest shareholder in ailing Nissan Motor Co., underscoring the weakening of industrial Japan. The deal is a risky venture for Renault, given Nissan's precarious financial status, which includes $21 billion in debt, according to Nissan. The agreement is a dramatic comedown for the company profiled by David Halberstam in his 1986 bestseller, "The Reckoning," as the symbol of the mighty Japanese auto industry.

But South Korea is perhaps the most tragic case of a once powerful Asian tiger being declawed. The following items are taken from a "Letter of Intent" dated May 2, 1998, from Chol-Hwan Chon, Governor of the Korean Central Bank, and Kyu-Sung Lee, Korean Minister of Finance, to Michel Camdessus, Managing Diretor of the IMF, that describes the policies Korea promises to implement in exchange for financial support from the IMF (the document is now available to the public on the IMF Web site):

Appoint outside experts to assist Privatization Committee to develop privatization strategy for Korea First Bank and Seoul Bank.

Select a lead manager for privatizing KFB and SB.

Obtain bids for KFB and SB by November 15, 1998.

Submit legislation to abolish regulations that prohibit foreigners from becoming bank managers by June 30, 1998.

Comprehensive review of all remaining restrictions on corporate foreign borrowing, including restrictions on borrowing of 1-3 year maturities, as part of review of Foreign Exchange Management Law to be completed by December 31, 1998.

Submit legislation to abolish restrictions on foreign ownership of land and real estate properties by June 30, 1998.

Increase the permitted equity ownership by foreigners of Korean telephone service providers from 33 to 49 percent by January 1, 1999.

Permit equity investment in nonlisted companies and eliminate aggregate ceiling on foreign investment in Korean equities by December 31, 1998.

Submit legislation to fully liberalize rules on takeovers of nonstrategic Korean corporations by foreign investors by eliminating the ceiling on the amount of stock foreigners can acquire without approval by a company's Board of Directors by June 30, 1998.

Permit foreigners to engage in securities dealings, insurance, leasing, and other property related businesses by April 1, 1998.

These concessions are astonishing for many reasons, not the least of which is that the question of foreign ownership has little or nothing to do with the Korean economic crisis or its resolution. Nicholas Kristof described some of the results of these and other concessions extracted by the IMF in "Asia's Doors Now Wide Open to American Business," in the *New York Times* on February 1, 1998.

In South Korea, as a direct result of the crisis, the government is talking about selling two of the biggest banks to foreigners, and teetering local securities firms are searching for foreign companies to take them over. Under an agreement with the monetary fund, foreign banks will be able to compete in Korea beginning this year, and the government is considering ways to ease the restrictions that prevent foreigners from buying Korean land. Walmart is studying whether to open outlets in the country.

For three decades South Korea had the highest rate of growth of GDP per capita of any country in the world. South Korea achieved these high rates of growth while preserving domestic ownership over its "world class" international business conglomerates, known as "chaebols." At the core of the highly successful "Korean model" were the ownership and financial links between large, modern industrial enterprises and Korean banks, and joint planning between Korean banks and various Korean government ministries. The "Korean model" is by no means unique—in most respects it is similar to the Japanese model that was equally successful in the 1950s, 1960s, and 1970s, and to the models of other successful Asian "tigers." Even before the crisis hit and the South Korean government was at the mercy of the IMF, it had begun to succumb to U.S. pressure to liberalize its financial sector. In the summer of 1996 the U.S. Treasury orchestrated a successful carrot-and-stick strategy to penetrate the South Korean economy. Nicholas Kristof reported in "How U.S. Wooed Asia to Let Cash Flow In" in the *New York Times* (February 16, 1999):

> After interagency discussions, the Administration dangled an attractive bait: if Korea gave in, it would be allowed to join the Organization for Economic Cooperation and Development, the club of industrialized nations.... The pressure on them is reflected in an internal three-page Treasury Department memorandum dated June 20, 1996. The memo lays out Treasury's negotiating position, listing "priority areas where Treasury is seeking further liberalization." These included letting foreigners buy domestic Korean bonds; letting Korean companies borrow abroad both short-term and long-term, and letting foreigners buy Korean stocks more easily. Such steps would help Korean companies gain more access to foreign loans and investment, but they would also make Korea more vulnerable to precisely the kind of panicky outflow of capital that unfolded at the end of 1997. Moreover, for all Washington's insistence that it emphasized building financial oversight, nowhere in the memo's three pages is there a hint that South Korea should improve its bank regulation or legal institutions. Rather, the goal is clearly to use the OECD as a way of prying open Korean markets—in part to win business for American banks and brokerages. "These areas are all of interest to the U.S. financial services community," the memo reads.

> In the end, Korea opened up the wrong way: it kept restrictions on long-term investments like buying Korean companies, but it dropped those on short-term money like bank loans, which could be pulled out quickly.

With hindsight it is easy for Kristof to see the danger in the choice Korea made. Indeed, with the same hindsight I explained in Chapter 5 how when Korean banks borrowed short-term internationally in dollars and lent long-term domestically in won the financial crisis triggered by the slowdown in export-led growth was aggravated. But it is easy to see what Korea was attempting to do: protect Korean companies and banks from being taken over by foreign owners, and keep Korean companies tied to Korean banks for loans instead of becoming dependent on international banks. In other words, in the summer of 1996 Korea was desperately fending off the U.S. attack team, and probably counted themselves lucky to get off with only the concession to open up for short-term international loans to Korean banks.

But after the crisis hit, the IMF upped the ante, and the struggle was over in weeks.

The IMF simply insisted that remaining restrictions on foreign ownership be rescinded and that the government take active steps to dismantle the chaebols as a condition of its bailout. As Sugawara explained in her *Washington Post* article on March 11, 1999:

In return for a massive rescue package, Korea's newly elected president, former dissident Kim Dae Jung, agreed to restructure the nation's closed and debt-ridden economy and embrace the free market. A key target of economic reform are the business groups, known as chaebols. The top five chaebols—Hyundai, Samsung, Daewoo, LG Group and SK Group—account for more than one-third of the country's gross economic output. Kim Dae Jung's new government launched a campaign to convince the nation that the chaebols, not foreign investors, were to blame for Korea's woes. Frustrated with chaebol foot-dragging, the government demanded that chaebols swap companies, an effort known as the "big deals." The big deals have drawn substantial criticism, especially after the government threatened to cut off bank credit to LG Group unless it agreed to sell its semiconductor subsidiary to Hyundai. "The big deals are idiotic. They will fail, because neither party wants to participate in these absurd arrangements, and in failing they will inflict considerable damage on the economy," said Stephen E. Marvin, head of research at Jardine Fleming Securities in Seoul.

If there is a czar of the South Korean reform effort, it is Lee Hun Jai, chairman of the Financial Supervisory Commission. The 55-year-old Lee, who has a master's degree in economics from Boston University, moved quickly after taking the reins of the commission last spring. Under Lee, the government seized a number of insolvent banks, closed five, and more significantly, agreed to sell Seoulbank to the London-based HSBC Holdings PLC and Korea First Bank to a US investment group led by Newbridge Capital Ltd. The government sought foreign buyers for these nationalized banks in hopes the newcomers would spur reforms. The same reasoning led the government to hire foreign fund managers to run a new Korean Development Bank. Also, Scudder, Kemper, Rothchild Inc., State Street Bank & Trust Co., and Templeton Asset Management Ltd. were chosen to manage the new $1.4 billion Corporate Restructuring Fund. Government officials contend this will force chaebols to reform. "The government will no longer be able to bail out the chaebols," declared Lee Hun Jai.

Many companies newly available for foreign purchase are very attractive to international investors not only because their stocks are depressed and the won is cheap, but because South Korean labor has been severely chastised. In April 1999 the Korean unions were waging a rear-guard action with the government of Kim Dae Jung and its neoliberal policies. Metal workers had joined public-sector workers on strike against layoffs. The Korean Confederation of Trade Unions described the situation as follows in a communiqué titled "Kim Dae Jung Government—The Mean Machine: Learning from Past Neoliberal Masters," issued April 24, 1999:

> On April 23 the government declared that it will dismiss all subway workers who refuse to return to work by 4 AM April 26. It referred to the US President Ronald Reagan's dismissal of 12,000 air controllers as the model for its action. It also announced that it will seek legal action to confiscate union assets and funds to cover the damages and loss incurred due to the strike. In this, the government invoked the example of Britain's ex-Prime Minister Margaret Thatcher. The escalation of the government's repressive attitude followed a meeting of ministers of so-called labor-related ministries, the Ministry of Finance and Economy, the Ministry of Justice, the Ministry of Local Government, and the Ministry of Labor. The decision to step up the hardline stance is reported to be based on the belief that "this is not a strike over wages or working conditions, but a political struggle" and that "there is a fear that if the government compromised now, the trade unions would try to intervene and interfere with each and every policy matter" (Chosun Ilbo, April 24, 1999). The government is believed to be prepared to arrest and imprison as many union leaders as needed.

One can only wonder how South Korean workers who demonstrated and occupied plants in their attempts to avoid massive layoffs at the hands of their fellow South Korean employers may react to going back to work for Western owners who flaunt their scorn for the South Korean system of "lifetime employment." Choo Won Suh, chairman of the Korean Federation of Bank and Financial Labor Unions, is clearly apprehensive:

> I hope that U.S. banks that acquire Korean banks will respect the culture and practices of Korean banks. I do not wish to speculate on how many Korean bank workers may be laid off after being taken over by a U.S. bank, but I am aware of the fact that layoffs will occur.

Finally, Nicholas Kristof worries about how Asians will react to what may quickly become the greatest American corporate takeover of all time (*New York Times,* February 1, 1998):

> One central question is whether an increasing American presence will spark antagonism toward the United States and the way it is seen as pushing its commercial interests as the price for throwing a lifeline to Asian economies…. The changes may set off alarm bells about economic colonialism.

He dutifully reports the standard excuse offered by every empire:

> The United States insists that the main beneficiaries of open markets will be local residents who will probably get new kinds of insurance and banks

that offer better service. The U.S. government insists that it is not a predatory beast forcing its companies on Asia, and many officials and outside economists alike argue that the policies of greater openness advocated by Washington are good for the countries on the receiving end. Although Washington pushed for more open markets, American officials say that effort has been secondary to the effort to bail those countries out. "Narrow self-interest was not a major element in our approach," said Stephen Bosworth, the U.S. ambassador to South Korea.

But, to his credit, Kristof also admits:

Not everyone agrees, and a U.S. business expansion in Asia has long been regarded as a nightmare by many nationalists in the region. Thus, for some nations trying to preserve their identity and autonomy, the American market-opening pressures smack of economic colonialism. "We must realize the great danger facing our country," Prime Minister Mahathir Mohamad of Malaysia declared in a televised speech a few days ago. "If we are not careful we will be recolonized."

In his article in the February 15, 1999, *New York Times,* Kristof offers an additional perceptive observation about international reactions:

Resentment at American policies—and perhaps, at America's economic success—has also led to a sense in many countries that the global economy is at an ideological turning point. In particular, there is a growing backlash against what some nations regard as an American model of laissez-faire capitalism, which rescues Connecticut hedge funds but sacrifices Indonesian children. Particularly in Tokyo and Paris, where markets have always been regarded as something like an ornery oxen—best when firmly yoked and even then prone to leave messes—there is talk of sturdier harnesses to guide capital flows, speculators and markets themselves.

If land swindles by banks and railroads in the U.S. West caught the eyes of "muckrakers" at the turn of the last century, one can only wonder what a new generation of international muckrakers will have to write about what may become the greatest international asset swindle of all time taking place right now, at the turn of the new millennium.

Notes

1. Edward Luce, "Top 10 Investment Banks Double Global Business," *Financial Times,* March 1, 1999. The top 10 banks are: Goldman Sachs, Morgan Stanley Dean Witter, Merrill Lynch, Salomon Smith Barney, Credit Suisse First Boston, Warburg Dillon Read, Deutsche Bank, J.P. Morgan, Chase Manhattan, and Lehman Brothers.

8 MAINSTREAM REFORM PROPOSALS
Evaluation

There are plenty of ideas and suggestions about how to reform the imperiled global economy, and some people are already busy educating themselves about them. For example, Ianthe Dugan informs us in "Gore Woos Wall Street" that Al Gore has been taking a crash course from Wall Street scions (*Washington Post,* January 11, 1999):

> When the Russian debt default threatened to destabilize world financial markets, the vice president wanted to understand the ramifications, so he invited a Wall Street "Who's Who" to the White House. Steven Rattner, chief executive of Lazard Freres & Co., John Tisch of Loews Corp., and money manager Orin Kramer helped organize this and similar meetings for Gore attended by "a strong list of powerful financial executives: global investor George Soros; Lionel Pincus of E.M. Warburg, Pincus & Co.; Bankers Trust Corp. Chief executive Frank Newman; Lehman Brothers Inc. chief executive Ricard Fuld; American International Group Inc. chief executive Hank Greenberg; Stan Schuman of Allen & Co.; and David Shaw, a former Columbia University computer science professor who runs a major investment pool in New York." The idea was to gather intelligence about how to stabilize world financial markets. "He asked us for our ideas," Shaw recalled. Jon Corzine, the co-chief executive of Goldman Sachs who is one of the biggest Democratic soft money donors ($380,000 in 1997–98), could not make the breakfast. But he went to Washington in the fall to meet Gore one-on-one for a half-hour chat over coffee. "The vice president has tried to understand how the global economy works from the eyes of someone sitting in Wall Street," Corzine said. "He wanted to understand the relative impact of the solutions, or lack of solutions, with respect to IMF funding, the Brazilian rescue and the Japanese stimulus package, and how they all fit together.

I am not privy to what his Wall Street mentors told him about the pros and cons of different reform proposals. But since the stakes are so great, I do not want to run the risk that our current vice (and perhaps future) president has not had the benefit of a full, unbiased tutorial, so I will explain and evaluate mainstream reform proposals for him and all other interested readers in this chapter.

Conventional Proposals to
"Make International Capital Markets More Efficient"
When real-world outcomes differ from the efficient ones predicted by mainstream models in textbooks, the memories of pro-capitalists are jogged to recall catch-all

phrases like "perfect competition" and "complete markets." The word "perfect" refers to knowledge and requires complete and accurate information for all participants in the economy about the consequences of all their conceivable choices, as well as accurate knowledge about all present and future prices for all goods and services. When someone points out that there is uncertainty in the real world, mainstream theoreticians only think of things like earthquakes and hurricanes, and redefine "perfect" to include accurate information about the probability distributions of uncertain events.

The word "competition" refers *not* to strategic behavior to best one's market opponents—which is what anyone grounded in the real economy would naturally assume—but instead to the number of buyers and sellers in markets. A competitive market is one in which there are a sufficient number of buyers so that no buyer can influence the price she must pay by deciding to buy more or less, and no seller can influence the price she receives by selling more or less. A "competitive" market is therefore one where all buyers and sellers are "price takers," and all attempts at collusion are doomed to failure. In other words, the competitive market of mainstream theory is precisely a market in which all "competitive" behavior is pointless, and therefore not to be expected! Markets are "complete" if there is a market for everything of consequence. Completeness refers to coverage, and requires that anything that anyone cares about can be bought or sold in a market—a perfectly competitive market, of course.

Once our capitalist visionaries remember that textbook predictions of full and efficient use of all productive resources (including labor) depend on the assumption that there are perfectly competitive markets for everything, as explained above, economic policy is straightforward and simple: reform the real world to conform more closely with the assumptions of the textbook models. Create new markets, generate more information, and add sellers and buyers to markets by clearing away obstacles to foreign participants. This is the logic behind conventional "new architecture" proposals, which are the standard remedies recommended by those who orchestrated international liberalization in the first place.

Calls for *greater transparency and disclosure* are almost universal. Requiring both public and private national financial institutions to collect and disclose better information regarding their own financial status and the status of those they lend to is called for so that depositors and investors are less likely to operate in blissful ignorance of negative developments, only to be jolted by unpleasant revelations when they become impossible to hide. *Improved prudential regulation* of banks and other financial institutions for developing countries is now recommended as a panacea, ironically by many of the same people who presided over deregulation of the financial sector in the U.S. and in Europe during the past 20 years. It's amazing how many see the wisdom of "prudential regulation" of financial markets after a crisis has hit, but recommend removal of "regulatory obstacles" to financial market "efficiency" when the credit system is running smoothly. No less an authority than Paul Volcker made this point in a luncheon address to the Overseas Development Council Conference on "Making Globalization Work" on March 18, 1999:

> I've been involved in financial supervision and regulation for about 40 of my 70 years, mostly on the regulatory and supervisory side but also on the side of those being regulated. I appreciate good banking and consistent accounting standards. But I have to tell you from long personal experience, bank regulators and supervisors are placed on a pedestal only in the *aftermath* of crises. In benign periods—in periods of boom and exuberance—banking supervision and banking regulations have very little political support and strong industry opposition—in developed and developing economies alike.

It is also amazing how easy it is to recommend more prudent financial regulation for others while backsliding on this issue oneself. In the May 2, 1998, "Letter of Intent" from the government of South Korea to the IMF, the list of concessions extracted regarding increased prudential regulation of South Korean banks and financial institutions runs more than two pages! But despite all the negative publicity about hedge funds that followed the collapse of Long Term Capital, and despite a high-profile Congressional investigation, Fed Chairman Alan Greenspan prevailed upon the Treasury-Federal Reserve special commission assigned to study the issue *not* to recommend new regulations on hedge funds. Hong Kong Monetary Authority chief executive Joseph Yam Chi-kwong responded to this decision in an address to the Institute of International Finance in Manila. As reported by Barry Porter in the *South China Morning Post,* May 3, 1999:

> Joseph Yam Chi-kwong has told the United States not to put the interests of American hedge funds and other highly leveraged institutions ahead of small open markets such as Hong Kong. He warned the US and other economic powerhouses against stalling proposed reforms to the world's financial architecture in the wake of the economic crisis. Mr. Yam told a gathering of leading international bankers that the many working groups set up to review possible global financial sector changes were taking "too long." "There is always the risk that, when the dust has settled, the initiative and enthusiasm, dare I say, on the part of those less affected by the crisis, may be stifled. There is also the risk that the plight of those who have been seriously affected by the crisis is not given the attention it deserves, simply because they do not have an adequately representative voice on the issues at hand at these international forums."

There is also a general consensus that *moral hazard must be reduced.* Moral hazard in the financial sector occurs when some actor behaves less prudently than she otherwise would because she will not suffer the full consequences of a misfortune. But the question is whose moral hazard, and how to reduce it. Some complain that IMF bailouts lead third world countries to borrow more dangerously than they otherwise would dare to, because they believe they can count on the IMF for emergency loans if need be. Others complain that IMF bailouts lead international investors to make riskier loans than they otherwise would, because they count on IMF bailout loans to those in their debt, which can be used to pay them off when their investments have gone sour. Still others complain that national banking policy traditions such as those in Japan, South Korea, and China encourage private banks in those countries to go further in debt than they otherwise would because they believe they can rely on governments to back them up in case of trouble, even if there has been no formal or legal underwriting agreement. And finally, many argue that an unintended side effect of government deposit insurance has been to eliminate monitoring of banking activities by depositors—who, if uninsured, would have more incentive to discipline risky banking practices by denying those banks their deposits.[*]

But there are sobering short-run economic costs to eliminating each of these practices that have, indeed, increased moral hazard. And there are long-run costs to consider as well. What will happen to people in the next third world economy that needs emergency international financial help if it is not given? What will prevent financial contagion from spreading to other economies deemed similar by international investors? What will prevent recessionary contagion from spreading from the economy that was not thrown a lifesaver to its trading partners? What will happen to the depositors as well as the stockholders in the next group of international banks, and what will happen to the shareholders in the next group of mutual funds whose international investments fall into default because no international relief effort is launched?

What will prevent contagion from spreading to other banks and mutual funds with extensive overseas investments? And what will prevent the ensuing financial crisis in the international investor economies from triggering an economic recession as those who lose their wealth consume less, and as financial institutions swamped with unexpected losses find it impossible to make new loans to perfectly healthy domestic businesses? Does not government deposit insurance reduce the

---

[*] Few within the mainstream bother to point out that the financial sector is, by definition, a leveraged credit system, and the more highly leveraged it is, the greater the moral hazard of any financial enterprise, since it bears less of the negative effect of any misfortune.

incentive for runs on banks? Does not government deposit insurance keep interest rates lower and thereby stimulate economic growth? Nor is private deposit insurance a panacea. If equally effective, it creates the same moral hazard as public deposit insurance does currently. But it is unlikely to be as effective because the key to effective deposit insurance is that the insurer be perceived as "too big to fail" itself—otherwise we simply have an infinite regress of depositor doubts. Since nobody bests Uncle Sam in the role of "too big to fail," private deposit insurance cannot discourage bank runs or lower the cost of borrowing as efficiently as government deposit insurance.

Calls for *better IMF surveillance* of borrowing countries and for making staff reports and minutes of IMF meetings public are now commonplace, as are suggestions for improved supervision in creditor countries. Another suggestion is to encourage private insurance companies to go into the business of selling insurance against international defaults to international investors. The idea is that international investors could invest in Russian government bonds, for example, and then take out an insurance policy on that investment, and the IMF would no longer need to intervene in the event of a Russian default to prevent financial panic in creditor nations' financial markets because investor losses would be covered. Proponents characterize this suggestion as creating a private market to replace a problematic public intervention. But notice, this "solution" does nothing for the Russian economy. It also does nothing for international investors who opt not to buy the (expensive) insurance. If there are enough who do not insure, the practical dilemma of whether or not to intervene remains, even if the moral case for allowing risk-takers to suffer losses is made even more compelling than it already is.

I agree with my colleague at American University, Professor Robert Blecker, when he offered the following evaluation of all these "conventional new architecture" proposals in his presentation on December 18, 1998, to the American University Conference on Globalization and Crisis: An Agenda for Action for the World Economy:[1]

> Most of these measures are helpful, but they are not sufficient to prevent financial crises or to lessen their impact on real economic performance. They are also not adequate for restoring high growth rates with full employment and broadly shared prosperity. We need different kinds of policies to make capital flows serve these objectives, rather than just to make capital markets work more efficiently and with less disruptions for wealthy investors.

However, I would add that if those who suggest these reforms offer them as alternatives to more far-reaching reforms—which they usually do—then they are not "helpful" but counterproductive to efforts to combat international inequity and prevent disruptions in the international credit system that cause terrible economic waste. And I would also point out that precious few of the alternative proposals coming out of the "Keynesian" side of the mainstream discussed below address the issues of international inequality and environmental destruction. Not surprisingly, they focus almost entirely on restoring financial stability and decreasing global disequilibrium.

Bring Back International Keynesianism

Within the mainstream, the battle is between neoliberal free-marketeers and a group of "new" international Keynesians who have recently found their voices. Prior to the outbreak of the Asian crisis, neoliberals were riding high on the wave of free market triumphalism, and the international Keynesians were a chastened lot. As a matter of fact, prior to the onset of the Asian crisis it was a rout, with Keynesians shedding identifying evidence like Jews and Moors once did during the Spanish Inquisition. But the international crisis put neoliberals on the defensive and heartened Keynesians who crawled out of the closet and went on the attack, full of suggestions about international economic reform. However, this is an old debate, and the proposals of the newly vocal international Keynesians are mostly old policies as well. Nonetheless, as usual, mainstream Keynesian policies are an improvement on policies based on a religious faith in markets despite all evidence to the contrary.

Most important, international Keynesians propose to *regulate capital flows*. There is too much hot money sloshing around the world. Most economists would cringe at this way of putting the issue, and insist on definitions for "too much," "hot," and "slosh." But that is the simple truth of the matter. Gerhard Schroeder, Germany's new Social Democratic chancellor, gave voice to this sentiment when he told a recent gathering of the world's economic *cognoscenti,* "If even George Soros—and he's a man who ought to know, having earned billions of dollars through speculation himself—urges us to introduce regulatory factors, it is high time for us to get down to some serious negotiation on a new international financial architecture" (*Toronto Globe and Mail,* February 2, 1999).

The best-known suggestion for discouraging speculation in foreign exchange markets is the *Tobin tax.* More than 20 years ago Nobel laureate James Tobin suggested something on the order of a tenth to a half of a percent tax on all foreign exchange transactions to discourage speculation in these markets. Opponents immediately pointed out that unless all countries agreed to the Tobin tax, those who did would be penalized by free riders. Critics also asked who would enforce and collect the tax, and argued that taxing one kind of international investment only creates incentives to turn to other forms of international speculation, thus "distorting" international investment markets and possibly driving speculation into even more socially counterproductive areas. Given the present volume of activity in foreign exchange markets, it is now generally conceded that a tax of this size would generate considerable revenue but would reduce the volume of foreign exchange transactions by only an insignificant amount. No doubt Jacques Melitz's proposal of a 100 percent tax on short-term foreign exchange transactions would be a significant deterrent, but opponents point out this is politically out of the question even if it were good economic policy. Since IMF assessments of member countries are both a practical problem (getting the U.S. Congress to ante up) and a source of inequity (forcing taxpayers to assume the risk of international lending while investors enjoy the benefits) the major attraction of a Tobin-like tax seems to me to be as a source of funds for international bailouts. Estimates are that a Tobin tax could generate between $100 billion and $200 billion a year, which could be used for international bailouts and/or interventions to stabilize currencies. Since it is the international investors who benefit from bailouts and currency speculation, why not at least raise the funds for bailouts and currency stabilization by taxing them instead of taxing ordinary citizens, as the present system effectively does?

Capital controls are far more likely to reduce speculative flows of short-term capital than are taxes on foreign exchange transactions. The Chilean government has placed a *reserve requirement on short-term inflows,* thereby discouraging international investment "quickies" and encouraging long-term investments not subject to any reserve requirement. Unlike countries that succumbed to the IMF's liberalization initiatives, China and India retain significant restrictions on foreign exchange transactions and foreign ownership of assets, and now Malaysia has reimposed restrictions. In the wake of the damage to the East Asian economies caused by massive outflows of foreign investment, a return to *restrictions on capital outflows* has gained popularity in third world circles. Others propose *risk-weighted capital charges* on mutual funds and pension plans in advanced economies that engage in international investments to discourage particularly risky foreign investments by uninsured parties.

It is very difficult for individual countries to consider restrictions on capital outflows without sparking a panic. And it is very difficult for individual countries to maintain restrictions without jeopardizing new international investment. Only if international organizations like the IMF and World Bank sanctioned capital controls and facilitate coordination among borrowing countries would controls have much chance of success. Of course, the IMF and World Bank long ago abandoned this role assigned them at Bretton Woods and persist in actively discouraging capital controls despite recent rhetorical genuflections. Their newly vocal international Keynesian critics recommend going back to the Bretton Woods system of internationally sanctioned capital controls by individual country governments. This is a necessary step to stabilize the global credit system. So it is an important short-run goal to press for international conditions that permit affected countries to deploy capital controls in their defense without courting disaster and punishment, for the borrowing countries can certainly not rely on governments in lending countries to solve the problem with restrictions on lenders. While proposals to impose prudential restrictions on capital outflows from industrialized countries through risk-weighted capital charges on mutual funds and pension plans abound, and restricting short-term capital inflows into the U.S. and other industrialized countries to discourage panic-driven capital flight to "safe havens" are discussed, it would be extremely "imprudent" for underdeveloped countries to wait for any of these programs to be implemented before enacting capital controls themselves.

Many international Keynesians now speak openly of *reforming international organizations*. There is such a thing as a fireable offense. In a world where people took responsibility for the consequences of their actions IMF Managing Director Michel Camdessus and his chief advisor, Stanley Fischer, would have resigned long ago. And if they were not honorable enough to submit their resignations, they should have been fired. But who would fire them? Clinton, Rubin & Co. have not even criticized the Fund, so why would they fire its directors? Even with James Wolfensohn and Joseph Stiglitz, the President and Chief Economist, respectively, of the IMF's "sister" institution, the World Bank, in open disagreement with the Fund over its outdated analysis and policies, the Clinton Administration has not even taken Camdessus and Fisher to the woodshed. One can only assume this is because Clinton, Rubin & Co. have not yet decided if they are unhappy with what the IMF continues to do. In any case, there is no sign that the Keynesian "B team" is about to be summoned to replace the "A Team" of free-market ideologues who have gotten us into this mess.

International organizations certainly need to be reformed, but if critics of globalization cannot even get its most visible managers taken to the woodshed, there is no reason to expect that serious and helpful reforms are yet on the horizon. Two longtime experts on East Asia who lie well within the mainstream have called for an Asian Monetary Fund. In the November 7, 1998, issue of the *Economist* Robert Wade and Frank Veneroso argue persuasively that the IMF is either blinded by free-market ideology or hostile to the successful Asian economic development model. In either case they point out that the Asian economies would have suffered far less had there been an Asian Monetary Fund that understood and was sympathetic to the Asian model to play the role of lender of last resort at the outset of the crisis. Wade and Veneroso are so pessimistic about the prospects of reforming the IMF that they recommend turning the Asian Development Bank into an Asian Monetary Fund to take over the IMF's neglected duties in the region. Japan was both able to put up the capital and willing to initiate such a venture, but the Japanese plan was vetoed by the IMF at the insistence of U.S. Assistant Treasury Secretary Lawrence Summers. In any case, it is obvious to any student of banking that in a highly leveraged credit system it is not only advantageous to the everyday functioning of the system to have a trusted and responsible lender of last resort, it is highly risky to operate without one—which is exactly what we have been doing. If I were advising Asian governments, I would certainly encourage them to act on Wade and Veneroso's recommendation. If I thought the financial backing were there for an African Monetary Fund, I would recommend it as well. And if I thought the Inter-American Development Bank could break away from U.S. dominance and obtain sufficient financing to play the role of lender of last resort for Latin America, I would support it, too.

Unfortunately, only the Asian Development Bank has any realistic chance of pursuing this reform for now, but this may soon happen. According to Anthony Rowley (*Business Time On Line,* Singapore, May 31, 1999):

> The Tokyo-based Asian Development Bank Institute is mounting a frontal assault on the tactics adopted by the IMF in dealing with the Asian financial crisis, and is promoting alternative approaches which it claims would minimize economic damage caused by IMF prescriptions. Some believe that the move may herald a revival of Japan's earlier proposal for an Asian Monetary Fund. Financial crises of the kind that have erupted across Asia "are of a new nature and require new policy responses," declares the recently appointed dean of the ADB Institute, Masaru Yoshitomi. One of these is the provision of "credible emergency financing from official sources, with less strings," he says in what amounts to a direct challenge to tight IMF conditionality.

A financial system without a central bank is an accident waiting to happen. So long as the global credit system operates without the equivalent of a *global central bank,* we are playing Russian roulette. Regulating financial institutions to prevent them from destructive speculative excesses and counter-cyclical monetary policy are necessary roles that central banks play. But we should be under no illusions that central banks are democratic or equitable institutions. They are largely immune from public opinion and influence from elected legislatures. They are secretive institutions that not only disenfranchise workers and consumers but usually prioritize the interests of bankers and investors over those of industrial capitalists. Of course we should demand that a global central bank be structured democratically and equitably—that borrowers be represented on a par with lenders, that poorer economies be represented on a par with wealthier ones—in a word, that representation be based on population, not wealth. There are dozens of proposals for a global central bank under various titles. The more progressive versions are by Jeremy Brecher and Tim Costello, Jane D'Arista and Tom Schlesinger, John Eatwell and Lance Taylor, Paul Davidson, and Grieve Smith. But we should be under no illusions about what kind of global central bank we could expect given today's political conditions. If one is created, it will look a lot more like the national central banks as they now are than like the democratic monetary authority of our dreams. When calling for a global central bank in today's context, we are calling for a biased tyrant to create minimal order out of chaos for lack of a better alternative, much as someone might dial 911 to a despised police department from the scene of a riot.

But the IMF cannot even be trusted to play this minimal role—even though its current management has recently hinted that it would be willing to do so, if asked. For there is no reason to believe the IMF leadership would not sit on its hands while financial contagion spread, even if it had "lender of last resort" status and sufficient means to stop the contagion. We certainly need an international lender of last resort. And we have every right to demand one that is equitable and democratic as well as competent and effective. But at a minimum we need an effective one, not a completely ineffective one, which is all that could possibly come out of the IMF unless it were completely reorganized and restaffed.

New ideas for *managing exchange rates* now abound. Under Bretton Woods we had fixed exchange rates. Since 1973 we have had flexible rates—broadly speaking. New proposals include perpetually fixed rates maintained by *independent currency boards* in developing countries and transition economies (Steve Hanke), *a three-way system of pegs* between the dollar, euro, and yen (Ronald McKinnon), *fixed real targets* managed by an international monetary clearing union (Paul Davidson), and *target zones with wide bands and crawling pegs* (John Williamson). In my view it is more important to implement some system of exchange-rate management quickly than to decide which version is settled on. None is perfect, none is foolproof, and the differences among them vis-à-vis democracy and equity are little. The essential ingredients to an effective system of managed exchange rates are: (1) a credible threat of massive intervention to deter speculation and (2) prevention of deviations that generate excessive trade imbalances. These will prove more possible to achieve the more speculative capital flows are diminished. Without capital controls, exchange-rate management will surely break down. But before either capital controls or an effective system of exchange-rate management can be implemented, opposition from free-market skeptics like Treasury Secretary Rubin must be overcome. Bring back the Keynesians!

The objective of *international macroeconomic policy coordination* is to diminish "beggar thy neighbor" monetary and fiscal policies that trigger global deflation and unemployment. Howard Wachtel proposes a plan in which treasury secretaries and the heads of central banks of the major economies meet to coordinate interest-rate reductions and fiscal stimulus when world demand is weak and interest-rate increases and fiscal restraint when inflationary pressures are great—with promises not to "cheat" to gain individual advantage. He argues that if only this were done, the problems of capital controls and exchange-rate management would be considerably lessened. John Williamson's plan focuses on coordinating interest rates while leaving countries' fiscal policies independent. His plan also relies more on formulas for determining a world average interest rate as well as country differentials, where the formulas would be agreed to in advance. Again, the differences vis-à-vis democracy and equity are minimal, and the trade-off between effectiveness and political viability is unclear. The important point is that individual-nation rationality regarding monetary and fiscal policies often proves globally counterproductive or irrational. Hence, some rough system of coordination can yield significant improvements over the current state of affairs. Once again, there is no reason for us not to shout: "Bring back the Keynesians. Any Keynesian!"

Progressive calls for *international debt relief* for humanitarian reasons fell on deaf ears for more than 15 years. Then, after the Asian crisis, some in the mainstream, like Jeffrey Sachs, also started to call for debt relief. On April 29, 1999, the *Washington Post* chastised the IMF, World Bank, and G-7 group of leading industrialized nations in an editorial titled "Real Help for the Poorest":

> Two and a half years ago the world's wealthiest nations agreed, after years of argument, on a plan to relieve the debts of the world's poorest nations.... Many nations owe so much money that even the wisest economic policies now will never rescue them from poverty. But the debt relief program hasn't worked. Too few countries have qualified, and those selected have received too little help.

Paul Blustein reported in the *Washington Post* on the following day that "Pope John Paul II, Archbishop Desmond Tutu and the rock group U2 agreed that next year, as the century draws to a close, the unpayable debts of the world's poorest countries should be forgiven."

What gives? Has everyone had a change of heart and joined Jubilee 2000, the umbrella organization of churches, labor unions, and organizations that champion the cause of the poor that has been spearheading the campaign for international debt relief? We can only hope so, but it is more likely that some have simply come to a hard-headed conclusion that without writing off some of the bad international debt it will prove impossible to restore order in the global credit system.

We don't need to ask whether or not they are correct in this assessment—that is an argument between new Keynesians, who think stabilizing the international credit system and reviving global demand requires significant debt relief, and new

Keynesians, who think stability can be achieved without "concessions." Progressives should make their support for other Keynesian reforms contingent on Keynesians' support for immediate, large-scale debt relief. But the fact that some of the "best and the brightest" mainstream economists now counsel "the powerful" that getting what they want—stability in global financial markets—cannot be achieved without debt relief does open discussion on an issue that had been taboo when only economic justice was at stake. Our job, of course, is to press to extend "strategically necessary" debt relief as far as possible into "equitable and humane" debt relief as well.

Notes

1. In Chapter 3 of *Taming Global Finance: A Better Architecture for Growth and Equity* (Economic Policy Institute, 1999) Blecker provides a more extensive evaluation largely consistent with the one presented here.

9 PROGRESSIVE REFORM PROPOSALS
Evaluation

We must first assume the International Keynesian B Team has properly sedated the international credit system, because $1.5 trillion of global wealth sloshing around the globe each day has truly become like the proverbial 900-pound gorilla that sits on any currency it wants and changes seats whenever a derivative tickles. As long as this is the case, whatever progress is made anywhere in the globe is in danger of being squashed when the whimsical gorilla ups to move and park its derrière on a different patch of national currency. But once this problem has been solved, how might globalization become progressive instead of reactionary?

Meaningful Debt Relief

In response to more than a decade of demands for humanitarian international debt relief, in 1996 the World Bank announced its initiative known as HIPC, for "highly indebted poor countries," that can only be considered a cruel joke. Only seven countries qualified, and of those seven only two met the further requirement imposed of six years of "sound economic performance" as judged by the IMF! By way of explanation why so little has been done to help so few, IMF Managing Director Michel Camdessus explained: "If we have learned one thing about debt relief, it is not so much that the amount of debt reduction matters.... What matters more is the quality and duration of the economic effort that must support the debt relief and create change for the better"[1]—by which Camdessus means, of course, how religiously the local government administers the IMF austerity formula. But as Carole Collins, U.S. coordinator for the Jubilee 2000 campaign explains: "The economic reforms required by the IMF and World Bank as a precondition for debt relief have a negative effect on poor people, because those reforms often deny them education or health care or increase the cost of those services."[2] Simple human decency and economic justice dictate immediate relief for a great deal of third world debt. Moreover, if conditions are to be attached, they should require governments seeking debt relief to adopt policies aimed at lifting people out of poverty— for example, pledging to spend all the savings from reduced debt payments on health and education. Olivio Dutra, who took office in January 1999 as the newly elected governor of Rio Grande do Sul, one of Brazil's most economically developed states (on the border with Argentina and Uruguay), is an example we should hope others will imitate. Brazilian state governments have increasingly used tax breaks and other forms of incentives to lure foreign investors in what some governors have nicknamed a "tax war." Dutra declared a unilateral cease-fire when he suspended $257 million in incentives for GM and Ford negotiated by his predecessor, targeting the money instead on ailing schools and hospitals. Dutra explained: "The decision is that not 1 percent of public funds will go to those who do not need it." And his Development Secretary, Jose Luiz Viana de Moraes, elaborated: "The government needs to invest in health, education, housing and security. We want those businesses to stay in Rio Grande do Sul, but under different contractual terms."[3]

Beyond debt relief for reasons of decency and justice, there is now a compelling case for international debt relief to get a number of economies started again. As long as Asian financial sectors are immobilized by bad debt, they are ineffective in giving the new loans necessary for investment, production, and employment to recover. The IMF strategy for solving this problem is to shut down insolvent Asian banks and permit international banks to buy up their depreciated loan assets while Asian depositors (or taxpayers, if there is government deposit insurance) pay the bill. An alternative way to reboot the credit system, and thereby the economy, is to enable existing Asian banks to make new loans by excusing them from paying a significant portion of their current international debt, or allowing them to unilaterally reschedule. Debt relief is like a quick "soft boot" compared with the slower IMF "hard boot," which is less equitable as well.

Labor and Environmental Standards:
Is That the Whole Issue?
Many progressives approach globalization intellectually by appending conditions on labor and environmental standards to mainstream proposals, legislation, and international treaties. While liberals counsel progressives to water down demands for international labor *standards* to labor *rights* to organize, many popular campaigns consist of fighting to put more teeth into rights and standards before agreements are signed, and fighting to enforce any rights and standards that are included. There is nothing wrong with this kind of work, and a great deal more of it is part of what is needed—especially when part of a broader movement to transform the global economy "from the bottom up." But I worry that those who work on campaigns to strengthen labor and environmental rights and standards deceive themselves about the limits of what can be accomplished through these means. I worry that they might lapse into thinking that if only labor and environmental standards were uniform internationally and sufficiently high, more free trade and international investment would be perfectly acceptable. I worry that not all understand that even if uniform international labor and environmental standards were set at any level one wishes to specify, more free trade and international investment would still increase global inequality.

Suppose working conditions, or "labor standards," were the same in all countries. And suppose environmental laws and regulations, or "standards," were the same in all countries as well. But suppose real wages were lower in some countries than others. If capital were mobile, businesses would move from high-wage countries to low-wage countries, depressing wages in the high-wage countries and increasing wages in the low-wage countries—assuming away the important offsetting effects in the low-wage countries like the destruction of traditional agriculture, as discussed in Chapter 2. Even if capital were not mobile, if we opened up free trade in goods between countries, businesses would specialize in producing capital-intensive goods in the high-wage countries and specialize in producing labor-intensive goods in the low-wage countries, also depressing wages in the high-wage countries and increasing wages in the low-wage countries—again, assuming away offsetting effects in the low-wage countries. So, unlike a world where national economies are isolated from one another so lower wages in one country have no effect on wages in other countries, international investment and trade create a mechanism through which lower wages in some countries will tend to depress wages in countries that have higher wages. But could workers in the high-wage countries respond to the downward pressure from free trade and investment by offering to accept reductions in their labor standards or in their environmental standards, rather than taking a money wage cut? Obviously they could, unless some international treaty prevented them from doing so. Their employers could care less about what kind of cost-reducing concession they make, just so the magnitude of the cost reduction is sufficient.

Which means that lower wages in third world economies not only put downward pressure on first world wages, they put downward pressure on first world labor and environmental standards as well when we engage in free-market trade and investment. Similarly, lower labor or environmental standards in the third world not only put downward pressure on first world labor or environmental standards, they put downward pressure on first world wages as well when we engage in free-market trade and investment.

More simply, any form of lower living standard in the third world that lowers the private cost to businesses of producing goods or services there puts downward pressure on all aspects of living standards in the first world under free-market trade and investment. So, raising labor standards or environmental standards in the third world is not only good in and of itself; it also diminishes the downward pressure on living standards in the first world from international capital flows and free trade. But it does just as much to alleviate downward pressure on wages as it does to protect first world labor or environmental standards. And raising third world wages is not only good in and of itself; it also diminishes downward pressure on living standards in the first world from free-market globalization. But raising third world wages does just as much to alleviate downward pressure on labor and environmental standards in the first world as it does to protect first world wages. Finally, if we actually established a uniform code of labor and environmental standards, then all differences in first and third world living standards would take the form of wage differences, and lower third world wages would of necessity exert all their downward pressure through international investment and trade on first world wages, since concessions in other aspects of first world living standards would be prohibited by international treaty.

The basic lesson here is that any distinctions people make between labor standards, environmental standards, and wages are artificial when we are dealing with the consequences of globalization and strategies to combat its pernicious effects. The issue is living standards and differences in living standards. When national economies are integrated through free markets, lower living standards in some countries make it more difficult to raise or preserve living standards in countries with higher living standards. Or, put differently, as long as there are differences in standards of living in different countries, making labor and environmental standards uniform throughout the world does not make the playing field even. It simply dictates that all of the unevenness will be squeezed into the part of living standards composed of wages instead of spread out over the entire field of living standards, which includes wages, labor standards, and environmental standards.

For this reason we should not limit our equity demands to creating uniform labor and environmental standards. Contrary to popular opinion, uniform standards would *not* create an "even playing field." It would merely force all of the inequality in international living standards to take the form of differences in wages, and it would mean that all of the downward pressure of lower third world wages would be brought to bear on first world wages. Uniform standards are only a partial program for improving global equity and an unwise retreat from a full program demanding equitable terms of trade and investment. The New International Economic Order (NIEO) campaign of the Non-Aligned Movement of the 1970s was in some ways a better framework for reducing international inequities. First of all, it focused (correctly) on the *result* we must insist on: that globalization reduce global inequalities. Second, the NIEO campaign started from the (correct) premise: as long as living standards are different in different countries, global inequalities can only be reduced if the terms of trade and international interest rates are set by negotiation rather than free-market forces.

On the other hand, the NIEO was seldom a "bottom up" movement, which proved to be a fatal weakness. It centered around the activities of progressive third world heads of state and their economic ministers, who were the ones who periodically "spoke to global economic power" in the form of speeches, communiqués, and resolutions adopted by international organizations dominated by third world governments—only to be ignored by all international organizations dominated by the first world. As a movement, efforts to fight for international labor and environmental standards in the 1980s and 1990s have been greatly superior to the NIEO of the 1970s because they have centered around the activities of grassroots organizations, unions, and independent institutes and coalitions, and because they have included first world as well as third world constituencies fighting for their own interests in solidarity with one another. Building the progressive response to reactionary globalization as a response "from the bottom up" by all constituencies negatively affected, together pursuing what Jeremy Brecher and Tim Costello call the "Lilliput Strategy," is *the* critical first step.[4] And so far the fight for international labor and environmental standards has been the center of this trend.

The international coalition that derailed the corporate-sponsored Multilateral Agreement on Investment (MAI) is an excellent example. Reginald Dale reported in the *International Herald Tribune* on March 5, 1999:

> As preparations get under way for a new round of international trade negotiations some of the world's top trade diplomats are haunted by a nightmare. It is that their jealously guarded privacy is about to be invaded by a horde of sandal-clad hippies accusing them of exploiting child labor, destroying the jobs of honest blue-collar workers, encouraging the slaughter of endangered sea turtles and other unspeakable horrors. These NGOs come in all shapes and sizes. Some of the more respectable groups are dedicated to widely shared objectives such as the fight against corruption or the relief of hunger. But many of the most militant NGOs have 1960s-flavored agendas of hostility to free trade and economic globalization. Those hostile to globalization have been vastly emboldened by their success last year in helping to kill the plan for a multilateral agreement on investment that was under negotiation. That marked the first time the NGOs had managed to influence the outcome of a major international economic negotiation—partly by making deft use of the Internet—and some senior trade officials now fear they could do the same to the Millennium Round of trade negotiations unless greater care is taken to prepare the political climate.

To Integrate or Not to Integrate: Is That the Question?

In an op-ed piece published in the January 26, 1999, *Washington Post* titled "The Trade Battle," E.J. Dionne Jr. provides insights about this debate that send chills down my spine.

> While everyone talks about history's verdict on Clinton and impeachment, the change in our approach to organizing the world's commerce bids to play a larger role in defining this era's historical legacy. Clinton hinted at this in his State of the Union message. "I think trade has divided us and divided Americans outside this chamber for too long," he told Congress.

"Somehow we have to find a common ground.... We have got to put a human face on the global economy." Clinton went on to embrace a new International Labor Organization initiative "to raise labor standards around the world" and pledged to work for a treaty "to ban abusive child labor everywhere in the world." He promised trade rules that would promote "the dignity of work and the rights of workers" and "protect the environment."

Behind these words is a battle that has been waged in Washington, largely out of public view, since the 1997 defeat of a bill that would have given Clinton the authority to negotiate trade treaties on a "fast track." The fast-track defeat demonstrated that liberal, pro-labor Democrats now have veto power over legislation to promote free trade and to support global economic institutions such as the World Bank and the International Monetary Fund. Without the liberals, there aren't enough votes in Congress to pass such initiatives. These pro-labor Democrats have used their newly found influence to push for more assistance to workers who are hurt by freer trade and for stronger international rules to protect workers' rights and the environment.

Rep. Barney Frank (D-Mass.) says the new situation can be explained by the division of Congress into three groups. There are, in his terms: (1) "isolationists" who are skeptical of all international institutions and free trade; (2) "trickle downers" who favor free trade and free markets but oppose any rules to regulate the global economy; and (3) "international New Dealers" who accept the global market as a reality but care passionately about lifting labor standards and wages, in the United States and elsewhere.

Because the "trickle downers" lack the votes to pass free trade or support international institutions on their own, they need the "New Dealers" to create a majority. The Clinton Administration, particularly Treasury Secretary Robert Rubin, came to realize this and opened negotiations last year with Frank and his allies—they include House Minority Whip David Bonior (D-Mich.) and Rep. Nancy Pelosi (D-Calif.). In October, Rubin sent a letter to Frank making important concessions in pursuit of the group's votes on new financing for the IMF. "I believe that one of the ways to build the confidence of workers is to seek the adoption and promotion of policies abroad that will enhance the respect for core labor standards," Rubin wrote. "The United States," he went on, "will work to affect the policy dialogue between the IMF and borrowing countries so that recipient countries commit to affording workers the right to free association and collective bargaining through unions of their choosing." Rubin also pledged to push the global financial institutions "to encourage sound environmental policies." Clinton's State of the Union pledges were the logical next step in this running negotiation. Frank saw Clinton's promise to work against "abusive child labor" as especially significant. "It's important for some of the labor people, and it's one of the most visible examples that you can do something" to regulate the workings of the global marketplace.

C. Fred Bergsten, director of the Institute for International Economics, thinks the trade debate has changed fundamentally. "Most trade types thought the merits of free trade were so obvious, the benefits were so clear, that you didn't have to worry about adjustments—you could just let the free market take care of it," he says. "The sheer political gains of the anti-globalization side in the last few years have made the free trade side realize that they have to do something to deal with the losers from free trade and the dislocations generated by globalization." This battle has only begun and the common ground that Clinton says he seeks could prove elusive. "The jury is still out," Frank says, referring to the administration's intentions. But creating a global economy that promotes growth with a measure of social justice is a big and worthy project—yes, the sort of thing that might matter more to historians than our current preoccupations [the impeachment trial].

Let's review. Round 1: In 1994 Congress passed NAFTA when Slick Willy sold trickle-down snake oil to enough international New Dealers—promising only a few trinkets that he later reneged on—to overcome the "nay" votes of conservative isolationists. Round 2: Enough snake-bit international New Dealers voted with the conservative isolationists to deny Willy fast-track authority—denying the slime meister a blank check and waiver of future Congressional rights regarding international economic policy. Round 3: Conservative isolationists have committed political suicide over the impeachment debacle, and Willy and the international New Dealers are now bosom buddies, having together repelled the Republican-attempted coup d'état via impeachment. Willy, Rubin & Co. are once again selling the same old snake oil, dangling the same old trinkets in front of their international New Deal allies in Congress, who assure us that they "care passionately about lifting labor standards and wages, in the United States and elsewhere."

The good news is, thanks to the negative effects of NAFTA on most Americans, thanks to the sobering effects of the greatest economic crisis since the Great Depression, thanks to the arrogance of the MAI managers, and thanks to the tireless efforts of the international grassroots anti-globalization network, "liberal, pro-labor Democrats now have veto power over legislation to promote free trade and to support global economic institutions such as the World Bank and the International Monetary Fund." The bad news is that "liberal, pro-labor Democrats now have veto power over legislation to promote free trade and support global economic institutions such as the World Bank and the International Monetary Fund." This is the bad news because they are notorious wimps and the last people in the world you would want to rely on when their feet get put to the fire. It is hard to imagine that anyone could believe that Clinton, Rubin & Co. would pressure the IMF to pressure governments of borrowing countries to improve their workers' living standards. But I am willing to bet that a number of liberal Democratic Representatives will sign off on a significant piece of international economic legislation before Clinton leaves office with only the fig leaf of a meaningless, unenforceable clause critical of "abusive child labor" (as if there were such a thing as "non-abusive child labor") to hold up over their shame.

But there is always hope. Representative Jesse Jackson Jr. abandoned his support for the African free trade bill called the African Growth and Opportunity Act, which passed the House but stalled in the Senate in 1998, after he learned how harmful it would be. He now refers to this bill as the African Recolonization Act and has introduced the African Human Rights, Opportunity, Partnership and Empowerment Act, or African HOPE, bill as an alternative. African HOPE is not only a good piece of legislation—for example, it calls for cancellation of sub-Saharan Africa's $230 billion unpayable debt—it already has the endorsement of 60 members of Congress, which is probably sufficient to send the corporate-sponsored bill to defeat once again. Broader in scope but not as far along the legislative track is a bill Representative Bernie Sanders intends to introduce called the Global Sustainable Development Resolution. While neither bill has any chance of passage in the near future, both serve to focus opposition to corporate-sponsored globalization in Congress and open debate on positive alternatives for the future.

The "Smart Set" Trap

Many progressives are understandably anxious to distinguish themselves from right-wing isolationists who eschew any concern for the well-being of foreign workers and oppose participation in any international organizations or treaties that limit the ability of the U.S. to act unilaterally. But allying with "liberal" globalizers who pay lip service to progressive goals, using the rationale that globalization *should* be beneficial, is a dangerous trap under present conditions. The unfortunate truth is that for the foreseeable future the balance of power in the U.S. government, in international economic organizations, in the mainstream media, between corporate America and labor, and between the rulers of the first world and the citizenry of the third world is extremely favorable to those who favor further *un*democratic, *in*equitable, environmentally *de*structive, and *in*efficient globalization, and extremely unfavorable to opponents of this unfolding disaster. This means that *for the foreseeable future desirable globalization is not possible.* We should not allow ourselves to be charmed by the sellers of trickle-down snake oil or deluded into believing any concessions they offer would be better than just stopping further globalization for the time being. This is a time for opponents of corporate-sponsored globalization to organize under the banner "Hell, no!" and threaten any who negotiate on our behalf if they capitulate and try to make us believe the fig leaf they bought for us is an adequate suit of clothes.

But this does not mean we who stubbornly oppose corporate-sponsored globalization—and that is what I recommend—are anti-globalization per se. This does not mean we deny that international investment and greater international specialization of production *can* be part of making the world a better place to live. We can and should present examples of trade agreements and conditions for international investment that would really yield efficiency gains and would really distribute those gains in a way that increases global equality and restores environmental balance. We can and should propose reforms in our international economic organizations that would make them more democratic and more effective managers of the global credit system, reducing the destructive economic disequilibrium it gives rise to. But we should be under no illusions that this kind of globalization will be accepted by those who, for the moment, hold the upper hand—be they A Teamers or the majority of those on the B Team. In other words, we should not be politically naive, and we should not deceive ourselves, just because the world's villages could be better off in a more highly integrated system of equitable cooperation, that permitting more global pillage is moving us in that direction.

Organizing from the Bottom Up

It is almost always more important to build the social movement correctly than to have the "correct" analysis or set of "demands." Organizing opposition to corporate-sponsored globalization "from the bottom up" is the right approach. Organizing all constituencies negatively affected to fight for their own interests while they learn why their own success necessarily hinges on the successes of other constituencies against whom global corporations will constantly pit them is the right approach. Incorporating first world constituencies together with third world constituencies in the campaign against the global "race to the bottom" is the right approach. Basing the movement on grassroots organizations, unions, and independent institutes and coalitions rather than principally on politicians and governments is the right approach. Adopting the "Lilliput strategy," where each constituency struggles to tie its own string to contain the "Gulliver" of global capital, knowing (correctly) how weak and vulnerable that single string is without the added strength of tens of thousands of similar strings, is the right approach. Our biggest advantage is that somehow the international movement against corporate-sponsored globalization has largely taken on this form. It is noticeably different from the movement for international economic justice of two decades ago in this crucial regard, and markedly superior. If there is some group of wise activists who deserve responsibility for this fortuitous turn of events, I would like to nominate them for the progressive movement equivalent of a Nobel Prize. And I would like to believe we have gotten off on the right foot through wisdom and perseverance of leaders who will continue to prove a valuable asset. But even if the improved composition, form, and strategy of the movement are largely accidental or the result of the disappearance of negative forms of leadership prevalent in the past, it is important to appreciate and nurture our one great advantage for the moment.

Recognizing that the current form of globalization is nothing more than a generalized downward leveling in which global corporations are extracting more and more of the wealth, power, and productive energies from communities and the environment is the right approach. Recognizing that our response must be nothing less than upward leveling that does entail the transfer of resources, power, wealth, and knowledge from the world's haves to the world's have-nots is the right approach. Recognizing that upward leveling, entailing redirecting productive resources toward the most important needs and preventing them from being allowed to languish or devoted to luxury or waste is the right approach. Recognizing that it takes a democratic movement to successfully combat the preemption of economic decision-making at the core of the reactionary globalization agenda—even if movement democracy must grow in a complicated shifting network characterized by the conflicting themes of autonomy within solidarity—is the right approach. And knowing that in every specific battle, what we are fighting for is merely the substitution of the human agenda for the corporate agenda is what can guide and sustain us.

Notes

1. Quoted by Paul Blustein in "Consensus Backs Relief for Poor Nations in Debt," *Washington Post*, April 30, 1999, E3.

2. Ibid.

3. "Brazil State Scraps Incentives for Ford, GM," Reuters, March 22, 1999.

4. Jeremy Brecher and Tim Costello, *Global Village or Global Pillage: Economic Reconstruction From the Bottom Up* (Cambridge, MA: South End Press, 1998), Chapter 6.

CONCLUSION
Lilliputian Luddites Until
Globalization Can Be Built from Below

What have we learned? How should we respond to corporate-sponsored globalization? Are there minimal demands to organize around?

- We know that under current conditions, globalization, even without crises, will continue to lead to more environmental destruction, greater global inequality, and less economic democracy in which the winners far outnumber the losers.

These were the results of international liberalization prior to the onset of the new period of global crisis that began in East Asia in the summer of 1997 (see Chapter 1). More corporate-sponsored globalization, even if immunized against crises, will replicate these results in the future more surely than it did during its infancy.

- We know the dramatically liberalized and extended international credit system not only increases the probability of crises and the likelihood of contagion; it is literally an accident waiting to happen—again and again.

Moreover, whenever a bubble does burst, it is perfectly capable of wiping out decades of economic growth in what had been one of the more fortunate "emerging market economies." This has already taken place in Thailand, Malaysia, Indonesia, and South Korea (see Chapter 3). As this book was written, a financial crisis had turned into a serious and deepening recession in Brazil, and Ecuador had gone from barely a blip on the international economic radar screen to full-blown crisis in less than a week. Moreover, it is quite likely that some new emerging-market economy will have made international headlines before this book appears because (1) even emerging market economies with relatively sound institutions, policies, and "fundamentals" have no means of repelling overexuberant international investors whose inflated expectations at some point prove difficult not to disappoint; (2) global deflation is ever more likely as only the U.S. economy is expanding, and global deflation is the death knell for export-led growth strategies; and (3) early attempts to remove the A Team have failed, and every single reform proposal from international Keynesians has been successfully stonewalled for the moment as further liberalization is once again the order of the day.

- While progressives should favor competent Keynesianism, we should know that no amount of B Team corrections of neoliberal globalization will prevent further environmental destruction, greater global inequality, and diminishing economic democracy and variety.

Not that the return of the B Team to power seems imminent. As I write this conclusion in late March 1999, the A Team has consolidated its hold on power and beaten back all recent B Team initiatives. While the A Team was visibly shaken in October and November 1998, it has recouped quickly and recently gone on the offensive; it is now the B Team that is in retreat. According to reports in the financial press, U.S. and European central bankers (who have extraordinary power under the European Union) managed to block efforts at the recent G-7 meetings to seriously consider "new architecture" to control financial markets. Ironically, U.S. Treasury Secretary Rubin dismissed these proposals "as a form of madness" because they would require the U.S. "to turn over economic decision-making power to an international organization"! In the end all B Team proposals—including even the mildest, such as French President Jacques Chirac's call for keeping the dollar, yen, and euro within zones—were tabled by the G-7 indefinitely and consigned to an innocuous ad hoc committee for further study. Meanwhile, any hopes that the new Social Democratic government in Germany would press the B Team agenda rather than ally with A Teamers Blair and Clinton were dashed when Oskar Lafontaine, Germany's left-wing finance minister, who was also chairman of its ruling party, resigned from both jobs on March 11, 1999, after Chancellor Gerhard Schroeder caved in to an ultimatum from top German business executives and bankers and announced to his cabinet that he would no longer tolerate "anti-business" attitudes in his government. And in the U.S., the fact that Richard Gephardt, who listens to the AFL-CIO on international economic policy and opposed granting Clinton fast-track authority, gave his early endorsement to A Team stalwart Al Gore for the Democratic presidential nomination does not bode well for the B Team agenda in Congress should Gore win the White House and Gephardt become Speaker of the House in November 2000.

But even *if* a spectacular economic crisis toppled the A Team and brought the B Team to power in Germany, Great Britain, the U.S., and the IMF (and it is increasingly apparent that this is what it would take given the strength of the A Team's hold on power), even *if* the full smorgasbord of B Team policies were implemented and the evil genies of global financial crises and deflation were banished back to their bottles and order were restored in the global economy, because international trade and investment would still be guided by market forces, increased globalization would still aggravate global inequalities and environmental destruction and alienate most people further from control over the decisions that affect their economic lives.

- We should know that only replacing the economics of competition and greed with the economics of equitable cooperation will guarantee a globalization that takes advantage of potential efficiency gains in ways that also promote environmental protection, international equity, economic democracy, and variety.

This is so because discovering countries' true social opportunity costs cannot even be done by relying on market prices that ignore significant externalities. This is so because setting terms of trade so as to distribute more of the benefits of specialization and trade to poorer economies requires discussion, negotiation, and cooperation—since market forces lead to terms of trade that aggravate international inequalities. This is so because interest rates on international loans must be tied to relative living standards in different countries—since market interest rates increase global inequality. This is so because managing common property resources like the atmosphere, oceans, and waterways requires restricting access through international cooperation and substituting a reasonable social rate-of-time discount for the average rate of profit—since free access and discounting based on profitability lead to overexploitation. This is so because even after harmonizing and raising international labor and environmental standards, international trade and investment will continue to aggravate inequalities among and within countries if the terms of trade and interest rates are left to market forces rather than being agreed to through equitable cooperation. All of which makes apparent how much must be accomplished before globalization can advance the causes of equity, democracy, solidarity, variety, and even efficiency. To pretend otherwise is to deceive ourselves, and is counterproductive. But as daunting as these tasks may seem at present, it is encouraging to know that globalization can ultimately be rendered useful!

- But for now, the crucial task is first to slow, and then turn back the march of corporate-sponsored globalization.

    Progressives must learn where to "draw lines in the sand." We must learn how to "just say no!" to legislation that further liberalizes the international economy and provides benefits primarily for global elites—particularly Western and U.S. capital. Contrary to the misleading myths of mainstream theory, *freer* trade and international investment *under today's conditions* advance mainly the interests of the exploiters and speculators while threatening the livelihoods of the global majority.

    This is why we must act like Lilliputian Luddites[1] first and stop corporate-sponsored globalization by any means necessary. After corporate hegemony and the present system of global pillage have been defeated, our Lilliputian movement can cease to act like Luddites and begin to build a system of international equitable cooperation from below.

- Finally, we should have learned by now that opposition to corporate-sponsored globalization must be organized from the bottom up, and should be based on grassroots organizations, unions, and independent institutes and coalitions from both the first and third world working democratically in flexible structures characterized by autonomy within solidarity.

The fact that the movement against corporate-sponsored globalization has largely taken this form over the past decade, and that constituencies increasingly rest their hopes on a Lilliput strategy in which only when other constituencies have also won their battles and tied their strings will it prove impossible for global capital to snap the string of any particular constituency, is our greatest advantage. This approach must be nurtured and promoted at all costs.

For now a reasonable list of demands includes:

(1) *No support for "fixing" the international credit system without debt relief.* In other words, if B Team mandarins and politicians want our public and political support for their proposals to regulate capital flows, reform international organizations, or coordinate macroeconomic policies, we should insist that they include significant debt relief as part of their proposals to stabilize the international credit system. It is unconscionable that in 1997 the IMF collected $643 million more in repayments than it provided in new loans to sub-Saharan Africa—the world's poorest and most hopelessly indebted region—and in 1998 collected $390 million more than it disbursed.

(2) *No support for B Teamers who do not support national controls on capital.* There are B Team mandarins and politicians calling for reforming international organizations, better coordination of macroeconomic policies, and some form of exchange-rate management who refuse to endorse any form of capital controls. There are others who support mild approaches to capital controls such as a small Tobin tax, but decline to endorse stronger restrictions chosen by sovereign governments and refuse to denounce measures taken by international organizations like the IMF to punish governments that implement strong capital controls. No useful purpose is served by allying ourselves with B Teamers of this ilk. No package of B Team reforms without significant capital controls has any hope of sedating the 900-pound gorilla of highly leveraged international finance capital threatening small economies and progressive-minded governments. Any who fail to support the right of sovereign governments to protect their economies from such a dangerous enemy by whatever means they deem necessary cannot be our ally.

(3) *No support for an international "lender of last resort" without guarantees that lenders will foot the bill for bailouts and borrowers will be fully represented.* There are no insurmountable technical difficulties in shifting the burden of paying for international defaults from taxpayers and ordinary citizens of less developed economies to international lenders. Make them pay insurance premiums. Collect $100 billion to $200 billion a year through a minuscule Tobin tax. Force the lenders who receive the bailout to extend new loans on favorable terms as a condition

for the bailout. There is no lack of means, only a lack of will. To merit our support, an international lender of last resort must pass this simple-minded equity test, at a minimum. And while no bank in the near future will be as democratic as we would want, at least debtors can be as fully represented as creditors in its governing structures, which should be a second minimal condition for our support.

(4) *Opposition to legislation or international treaties regarding trade, direct foreign investment, or international lending that do not pass the equity test: i.e., increased international economic activities must decrease, not increase, global inequality.* This condition will in all likelihood mean that we must oppose most measures globalizers will propose in the near future. Even sweetened by concessions regarding labor and environmental rights and standards, or trade adjustment benefits and retraining, it is unlikely that much legislation that increases globalization will pass this test in the near future.

Commodity prices overall lost 16 percent of their value in 1998 alone, continuing a long-term trend. Since these constitute the bulk of third world exports, expanding trade as the terms of trade continue to turn against the poorer economies is a recipe for increasing global inequality and quite possibly absolute poverty as well.

(5) *No expulsion of third world peasants from the land and no foreign ownership of land.* Instead, the most effective road to improving living standards for the worst-off global citizens, and therefore also the most effective way to arrest the race to the bottom for others, is radical land reform in developing economies and increases in the provision of economic, educational, cultural, and health services in rural areas. Not only is increasing the productivity and self-sufficiency of third world farmers critical to reversing environmental degradation due to modern export-oriented agriculture and incursions into forests by landless peasants; as we begin the new millennium, it is still the single most effective means for reducing economic inequality between third and first world economies, and within both third and first world economies as well.

Notes

1. The Luddites were a militant movement of workers who opposed early 19th-century capitalism in Great Britain. One of their many tactics was to destroy the machinery of their most recalcitrant employers. Too often modern progressives have accepted the view that the Luddites were backward-looking and destructive, which simply parrots the propaganda spread about them by their contemporary capitalist enemies. In fact, it was the early British capitalists who were reactionary and destructive when they refused to share the efficiency gains from mechanized production with their employees. The Luddites deserved a better fate then and deserve a better fate today. They should be remembered as heroic examples of what must sometimes be done when the powers that be stubbornly persist in imposing changes that spell ruin for the majority under the banner of increased efficiency.

APPENDIX A THE CONVENTIONAL VIEW
Why International Trade
Could Be Beneficial

When we use scarce productive resources to make one good, those resources are not available to make another good. That is the sense in which economists say there are *opportunity costs* of making goods. The opportunity cost of making a unit of Good A, for example, can be measured as the number of units of Good B we must forgo because we used the resources to make the unit of A instead of using them to make B. Opportunity costs are important for understanding the logic of international trade because whenever the opportunity costs of producing goods are different in different countries, there *can* be positive benefits from specialization and trade. And as long as the terms of trade are such that they distribute part of the benefit of specialization to both countries, trade can be beneficial to both trading partners.

For example, if by moving productive resources from the shirt industry to the tool industry in the U.S., shirt production falls by 4 shirts for every additional tool produced, while moving resources from the shirt industry to the tool industry in Mexico results in a drop of 8 shirts for every new tool produced; then the opportunity cost of a tool in the U.S. is 4 shirts, while the opportunity cost of a tool in Mexico is 8 shirts. If the international terms of trade were 6 shirts for one tool, the U.S. would be better off producing only tools—trading tools for any shirts it wanted to consume—and Mexico would be better off producing only shirts—trading shirts for any tools it wanted. This is because instead of using the resources necessary to produce 4 shirts, the U.S. could instead produce 1 tool and then trade the tool for 6 shirts. So the U.S. is always better off using its resources to produce tools and never shirts. And instead of using the resources necessary to produce 1 tool, Mexico could instead produce 8 shirts and trade the 8 shirts for 1 1/3 tools. So Mexico is always better off using its resources to produce shirts and never tools.

But 6 shirts for 1 tool is not the only conceivable terms of trade that would produce efficiency gains and benefits for both Mexico and the U.S. If the terms of trade were 4.1 shirts for 1 tool, both the U.S. and Mexico would be better off from specialization and trade. But in this case very little of the benefit would go to the U.S. Under these terms, trade allows the U.S. to get 4.1 shirts for 1 tool. But without trade the U.S. could get 4 shirts for each tool by shifting labor from the tool industry to the shirt industry. So the U.S. gains very little. However, Mexico gains a great deal when the terms of trade are 4.1 shirts for 1 tool. Instead of having to give up 8 shirts to get a tool by moving labor from the shirt industry to the tool industry, Mexico has to give up only 4.1 shirts to get a tool through trade. Mexico would like the international terms of trade to be as close to the U.S. opportunity cost of tools, 4 shirts for a tool, as possible. On the other hand, if the terms of trade were 7.9 shirts for 1 tool, the lion's share of the benefit from trade would go to the U.S. and very little to Mexico. Without trade Mexico can get 1 tool for 8 shirts simply by reallocating labor. Having to give up only 7.9 shirts instead of 8 to get a tool is a modest gain. But at these terms, trade allows the U.S. to get 7.9 shirts for every tool whereas without trade the U.S. could get only 4 shirts for every tool by moving labor from its tool industry to its shirt industry. The U.S. would like the international terms of trade to be as close to the Mexican opportunity cost of tools as possible.

When David Ricardo explained the logic of *comparative advantage* in his *Principles of Political Economy and Taxation* in 1821 he was not particularly concerned with *why* opportunity costs might be different in different countries. Instead, he was anxious to demonstrate that even if one country was more productive in the production of both goods, that is, even if one country had an *absolute advantage* in the production of both goods, the more productive country could still gain by importing the good in which it was relatively, or comparatively, less productive, and exporting the good in which it enjoyed a relative, or comparative, advantage. In the example above, the U.S. might have been more productive in both tool and shirt production. Suppose it took only 1 hour of labor to make either 1 tool or 4 shirts in the U.S., but it took 10 hours of labor to make 1 tool or 8 shirts in Mexico. In that case the U.S. would be more productive than Mexico in producing *both* tools and shirts, and would enjoy an *absolute* advantage in both industries. But the conclusion we derived above, that the U.S. should specialize in tool production and import shirts from Mexico while Mexico specializes in shirt production and imports tools from the U.S., holds nonetheless. In other words, Ricardo was concerned to show that differences in opportunity costs were a sufficient condition for mutually beneficial trade, and therefore comparative, rather than absolute, advantage was the determining factor in what countries should and should not produce.

Trade theory since Ricardo has elaborated a number of reasons why opportunity costs differ between countries. Differences in climate or soil are obvious reasons countries might differ in their abilities to produce agricultural goods. Differences in the accessibility of deposits of natural resources are obvious reasons for differences in the opportunity costs of producing oil, coal, gas, and different minerals in different countries. And differences in technological know-how obviously give rise to differences in opportunity costs of producing manufactured goods. A more subtle source of differences in opportunity costs is different factor endowments. Even if technologies are identical in two countries, and even if the quality of each productive resource is the same, if countries possess productive factors in different proportions, the opportunity costs of producing final goods will often differ—giving rise to potential benefits from trade.

APPENDIX B

THE POLITICAL ECONOMY VIEW
Why International Trade *Will* Increase Global Inequality

The logic of comparative advantage—which teaches that all countries benefit from trade and none lose—and the reality of international trade—which keeps widening the gap between rich and poor countries—seem hard to reconcile. A simple model of North-South relations explains the conundrum.

A Simple Model of North-South Trade

There are two kinds of countries—Northern countries and Southern countries—and we assume there are so many of each that the international markets where goods are traded between countries are perfectly competitive. Each country, whether Northern or Southern, has 1,000 inhabitants, each of whom must have 1 unit of Corn to eat at year's end—after which people simply want to work as little as possible. There are two ways to make corn. One way uses only labor, the other way uses both labor and machines. There is only one way to make machines, requiring both labor and machines. The three technologies—two for making corn, and one for making machines—are as follows:

> 5 units of Labor + 0 Machines yields 10 units of Corn
>
> 2 units of Labor + 1 Machine yields 10 units of Corn
>
> 1 unit of Labor + 2 Machines yields 10 Machines

All Northern and Southern countries know how to use all three technologies. The only difference between the Southern and Northern countries is that each Northern country has 200 machines to start with, while each Southern country has only 50 machines to start with. We assume machines last one year, and require countries to replace any machines they use up during the year as well as obtain 1,000 units of corn so each citizen has one to eat. First we ask what each Northern and Southern country would do if it were not permitted to trade. Then we ask what would happen if we opened up trade and countries were free to trade corn for machines with one another. Finally, we ask if there are any conceivable terms of trade that would eliminate international inequality. I call the first solution the autarkic solution, the second solution the free trade solution, and the third solution the fair trade solution.

The Autarkic Solution

What would countries in each region do if trade were not permitted?

Making corn using machines as well as labor is more productive than making corn using labor alone even if you have to replace the machines you use up. It is more productive in the sense that you can get a given amount of corn with less labor using machines than not using machines. With 200 machines available the Northern countries do not have to use the less productive corn-making technology at all. If we let $X(1)$ be the number of times a country uses the technology for making corn via labor only, $X(2)$ be the number of times a country uses the technology for producing corn with labor and machines, and $X(3)$ be the number of times a country uses the technology for making machines, then even if a country replaces all machines used up in production during the year, Northern countries can produce all the corn they need to eat and replace all the machines used up to do it, expending the least amount of labor possible with the following production plan:

A Northern Country's Optimal Production Plan Under Autarky

$\quad\quad X(1) = 0$ using $M(1) = 0$ and $L(1) = 0$ to get 0 C

$\quad\quad X(2) = 100$ using $M(2) = 100$ and $L(2) = 200$ to get $1{,}000$ C

$\quad\quad X(3) = 12.5$ using $M(3) = 25$ and $L(3) = 12.5$ to get 125 M

This plan requires

$\quad\quad M(1) + M(2) + M(3) = 0 + 100 + 25 = 125$ machines

initially, which is less than the 200 each Northern country has to start with, and replaces the 125 machines used up. It uses a total of

$\quad\quad L(1) + L(2) + L(3) = 0 + 200 + 12.5 = 212.5$ units of labor

to get the 1,000 units of corn needed.

Notice that while this plan minimizes the labor expended (212.5 units to get 1,000 units of C), it does not use all of the machines available to each Northern country. It uses only 125 of the 200 machines each country has. But without trade, each Northern country must produce 1,000 C, which can be done with the least labor by making $X(1) = 0$ and $X(2) = 100$. And with $X(2) = 100$, $X(3)$ must $= 12.5$ to replace all the machines that will be used up. With $X(2) = 100$ and $X(3) = 12.5$, only 125 machines are required. There simply is no way for Northern countries to profitably use all 200 machines they have initially. And if trade is prohibited, the 75 unused machines in each Northern country cannot be used in Southern countries either.

Southern countries can make some of their corn the more productive way using machines because they also have some machines to start with. But with only 50 machines, and the requirement that machines be replaced if they are used, the most any Southern country can use the more efficient way of making corn using machines is $X(2) = 40$, in which case $X(3)$ must $= 5$. Since this yields only 400 units of corn, Southern countries will still have to use the less efficient technique for making corn with labor only, so $X(1) = 60$. Which gives us the following plan:

A Southern Country's Optimal Production Plan Under Autarky

X(1) = 60 using M(1) = 0 and L(1) = 300 to get 600 C

X(2) = 40 using M(2) = 40 and L(2) = 80 to get 400 C

X(3) = 5 using M(3) = 10 and L(3) = 5 to get 50 M

This provides 600C + 400C = 1,000 units of corn for consumption; uses exactly

M(1) + M(2) + M(3) = 0 + 40 + 10 = 50 machines,

which each country has initially; replaces all 50 machines used up; and does all this with the minimum expenditure of labor:

L(1) + L(2) + L(3) = 300 + 80 + 5 = 385 units of labor.

Since the citizens of all countries are consuming the same amount of corn and all machines used get exactly replaced, the only differences between outcomes in different countries is in average work times. This allows us to measure global inequality simply as differences in the average amount of work citizens of Southern countries must do compared with citizens of Northern countries. We define the *degree of global inequality* as the ratio of the number of days worked on average in the Southern countries divided by the number of days worked on average in the Northern countries. If Northern and Southern workers work the same amount, on average, the ratio will be 1. The more Southern workers have to work compared with their Northern counterparts, the higher will be the ratio and our degree of inequality. In the autarkic solution Southerners work 0.385 units of labor on average while Northerners only work 0.2125 units on average, and the degree of exploitation is therefore 0.385 / 0.2125 = 1.81. In this case the inequality is clearly the result of unequal initial endowments of machines, since both regions have access to the same technologies. But notice there is no social relation that serves as a transmission mechanism for inequality under autarky since the Northern and Southern economies have no relations with one another at all.

The Free Trade Solution

If we open up international trade for corn and machines and leave the terms of trade to be determined by the law of supply and demand in the international marketplace, what will the terms of trade turn out to be?

The only reason to want a machine is because it makes it possible to produce corn with less labor. Therefore, we can calculate how many units of corn anyone would give up for a machine as follows: Suppose we had 17 units of labor. Without machines we would have to use the less efficient technology for making corn that uses labor only, and we could produce 34 C with 17 L. On the other hand, if we had 10 machines we could use the more efficient technology for producing corn using machines as well as labor—although we would have to replace the 10 machines used up. 1 unit of labor along with 2 machines is sufficient to replace the 10 machines used up. That leaves 16 units of labor and 8 machines to produce corn the more productive way. 16 L and 8 M will produce 80 units of corn. So having 10 machines permits production of 80 - 34 = 46 more units of corn, and each machine, therefore, permits production of 46 / 10 = 4.6 more units of corn than would have been possible without it.

It is not worth paying more than 4.6 units of corn for a machine, because any country that did so would end up with less corn for a given expenditure of its labor. On the other hand, if the price of machines were less than 4.6 units of corn, countries would keep buying machines indefinitely since they would expend less labor per unit of corn by doing so. This implies the *equilibrium* price of a machine, P(M), is 4.6 units of corn, i.e., if left to competitive market forces, machines would sell for 4.6 units of corn each.[1] Now we are ready to see what will happen if Northern and Southern countries are free to trade machines and corn at these equilibrium terms of trade.

Each Northern country can get 1,000 units of corn to eat with the least labor expended with the following production/trade plan:

A Northern Country's Optimal Production Plan Under Free Trade

$X(1) = 0$ using $M(1) = 0$ and $L(1) = 0$ to get 0 C
$X(2) = 14.815$ using $M(2) = 14.815$ and $L(2) = 29.63$ to get 148.15 C
$X(3) = 25$ using $M(3) = 50$ and $L(3) = 25$ to get 250 M

Each Northern country expends 29.63 + 25 = 54.63 units of labor, uses 14.815 + 50 = 64.815 machines, and produces 148.15 units of corn and 250 machines.

A Northern Country's Optimal Trade Plan Under Free Trade

Export 250 - 64.815 = 185.185 M
Import 1,000 - 148.15 = 851.85 C

Since 185.185(4.6) = 851.85, each Northern country will have just enough machines to export in order to import the corn it requires.[2]

Each Southern country can get 1,000 units of corn to eat with the least labor expended with the following production/trade plan:

A Southern Country's Optimal Production Plan Under Free Trade

$X(1) = 0$ using $M(1) = 0$ and $L(1) = 0$ to get 0 C
$X(2) = 185.185$ using $M(2) = 185.185$ and $L(2) = 370.37$ to get 1851.85 C
$X(3) = 0$ using $M(3) = 0$ and $L(3) = 0$ to get 0 M

Each Southern country expends 370.37 units of labor, uses 185.185 machines, and produces 1851.85 units of corn.

A Southern Country's Optimal Trade Plan Under Free Trade

Export 1851.85 - 1,000 = 851.85 C

Import 185.185 M

Since 851.85 / 4.6 = 185.185, each Southern country will have just enough corn to export in order to import the machines it requires.[3]

The average work time in Southern countries is now 0.37037 while the average work time in Northern countries is now 0.05463. So the degree of global inequality has risen from 1.81 under autarky to 0.37037 / 0.05463 = 6.78 under free trade. Free trade increases global inequality in our simple model because it distributes the lion's share of the benefit of improved efficiency in the world economy to the Northern countries rather than to the Southern countries. We can compare the efficiency of the two solutions by comparing the combined number of units of labor worked in a Northern and Southern country. Under autarky the citizens of a Northern country work 212.5 units of labor and the citizens of a Southern country work 385 units of labor, for a total of 597.5 units of labor worked to produce 2,000 units of corn. In the free trade solution 54.63 units of labor are worked in the North while 370.37 units are worked in the South, for a total of only 425 units of labor worked to produce 2,000 units of corn. In both solutions all machines used were replaced, so opening trade produced an efficiency gain of 597.5 - 425 = 172.5 units of labor saved in the two countries together. But free market terms of trade give the Northern countries 157.87 units of the labor saved, reducing their work time from 212.5 to 54.63, and give the Southern countries only 14.63 units of the labor saved, reducing their work time from 385 to 370.37. And this was *not* because there were "imperfections" in the international markets for machines and corn. Quite the contrary, we granted the international markets every benefit of the doubt by assuming they reached their equilibrium price, and by assuming they were competitive, with no monopolistic advantage enjoyed by the North.

The Fair Trade Solution

How could we use international trade to simultaneously eliminate international exploitation and inefficiency?

If we allowed Northern countries to trade machines to Southern countries for 0.5882 units of corn per machine, inefficiency in the world economy would be completely eliminated, the Northern countries would end up no worse off than under autarky, and the Southern countries would end up considerably better off, working no more, on average, than Northerners for their corn.

At the terms of trade P(M) / P(C) = 0.5882, each Northern country can get 1,000 units of corn to eat with the least labor expended with the following production/trade plan:

A Northern Country's Optimal Production Plan Under Fair Trade

X(1) = 0 using M(1) = 0 and L(1) = 0 to get 0 C

X(2) = 93.75 using M(2) = 93.75 and L(2) = 187.5 to get 937.5 C

X(3) = 25 using M(3) = 50 and L(3) = 25 to get 250 M

Each Northern country expends 187.5 + 25 = 212.5 units of labor, uses 93.75 + 50 = 143.75 machines, and produces 937.5 units of corn and 250 machines.

A Northern Country's Optimal Trade Plan Under Fair Trade

Export 250 - 143.75 = 106.25 M

Import 1,000 - 937.5 = 62.5 C

Since 106.25(0.5882) = 62.5, each Northern country will have just enough machines to export in order to import the corn it requires.[4]

With P(M) / P(C) = 0.5882, each Southern country can get 1,000 units of corn to eat with the least labor expended with the following production/trade plan:

A Southern Country's Optimal Production Plan Under Fair Trade

X(1) = 0 using M(1) = 0 and L(1) = 0 to get 0 C

X(2) = 106.25 using M(2) = 106.25 and L(2) = 212.5 to get 1062.5 C

X(3) = 0 using M(3) = 0 and L(3) = 0 to get 0 M

Each Southern country expends 212.5 units of labor, uses 106.25 machines, and produces 1062.5 units of corn.

A Southern Country's Optimal Trade Plan Under Fair Trade

Export 1062.5 - 1,000 = 62.5 C

Import 106.25 M

Since 62.5 / (0.5882) = 106.25, each Southern country will have just enough corn to export in order to import the machines it requires.[5]

In this case, trade also permits the Southern countries to make productive use of the 75 extra machines each Northern country has, which remain idle under autarky. As a result the fair trade solution yields the same global efficiency gain— saving 172.5 units of labor, as did free trade. But in this case all of the efficiency gain is awarded to the Southern countries—reducing their work time from 385 to 212.5. While the Northern countries receive none of the efficiency gain, they are no worse off for trade since they worked 212.5 units of labor under autarky as well, and fair trade has completely eliminated global inequality—reducing the degree of global inequality from 1.81 under autarky to 0.2125 / 0.2125 = 1 under fair trade.

In sum, both fair and free terms of trade improve the efficiency of the economy to the same extent. Differences in the terms of trade merely distribute the benefits of the increased efficiency differently. Fair terms of trade can eliminate global inequality, or at least lower the degree of global inequality, by allowing the less developed countries to capture a larger share of the increased efficiency that results from specialization and trade. The fact that we can calculate fair terms of trade that would diminish international inequality while improving efficiency demonstrates that one does not have to retreat to autarky to avoid increasing international inequality through international trade. Trade can be arranged between countries to benefit both countries *and* reduce inequalities between them. But as long as the terms of international trade are determined according to the laws of supply and demand in free markets, our free trade solution demonstrates that there is every reason to expect international trade to increase the degree of global inequality compared with what it would have been under autarky. So the conventional view of international trade yielding global efficiency gains and providing mutual benefits is not inconsistent with the political economy view of international trade as a vehicle for increasing international inequalities after all.

Finally, we can use the model to calculate the effects of technical change on global efficiency and international inequality. If the productivity of the less productive technology for producing corn with labor only increases, global inequality will decrease. Interestingly, it will do so whether or not it improves global efficiency, which depends on whether there are sufficient machines in the world to avoid using the less efficient technology—in which case global efficiency would stay the same—or there are not sufficient machines to avoid use of the less efficient technology—in which case improving the efficiency of this technology obviously raises global efficiency. If we increase the productivity of either the more productive technology for making corn using machines along with labor, or the machine-making technology, global efficiency will improve, but global inequality will increase as well. These results do not depend on whether the technological change in making corn or machines, using machines and labor, is output-increasing, machine-saving, or labor-saving. So our model suggests that if technical change is more rapid in capital-intensive sectors than in labor-intensive sectors, this could be one reason global inequality is rising.

Notes
1. Notice there is *no* non-competitive market structure in our model. In particular, we assume *no* advantage for the sellers of machines compared with the sellers of corn due to either relatively fewer sellers of machines than corn in international markets or to differences in the elasticities of demand for the two products. Therefore, any inequality in our results does *not* stem from these well-known and much-studied causes.

2. The Northern countries cannot deliver all 185.185 M they export at the beginning of the year. If they did, they would be left with 200 - 185.185 = 14.015 machines to use for

production during the year, and they need 64.815 machines to carry out their production plan. But they can deliver 200 - 64.815 = 135.185 M at the beginning of the year and the remaining 50 M at the end of the year out of the 250 M they produce during the year. As we see below, this delivery schedule meets the Southern countries' needs since they need 185.185 M to carry out their optimal production plan, but they only need 135.185 delivered at the beginning of the year since they have 50 M of their own. When the Northern countries deliver the remaining 50 M at the end of the year the Southern countries can use those machines to replace their own 50 machines that were used up.

3. While the Southern countries can deliver all 851.85 units of their corn exports at the end of the year, they require delivery of part of their machine imports at the beginning of the year. They have only 50 M of their own but need 185.185 M to carry out their optimal production plan. So they need 185.185 - 50 = 135.185 M delivered at the beginning of the year. As we saw above, the Northern countries can deliver exactly that amount at the beginning of the year, and deliver the remaining 50 M at year's end.

4. Again, Northern countries cannot deliver all 106.25 M they export at the beginning of the year, since they would be left with 200 - 106.25 = 93.75 machines for production, and they need 143.75 machines to carry out their production plan. But they can deliver 200 - 143.75 = 56.25 M at the beginning of the year and the remaining 50 M at the end of the year out of the 250 M they produce during the year. This delivery schedule meets the Southern countries' needs, since they need 106.25 M to carry out their optimal production plan, but they need only 56.25 M delivered at the beginning of the year since they have 50 M of their own. When the Northern countries deliver the remaining 50 M at the end of the year, the Southern countries can use those machines to replace their own 50 machines that were used up.

5. While the Southern countries can deliver all 62.5 units of their corn exports at the end of the year, they require delivery of part of their machine imports at the beginning of the year. They need 106.25 - 50 = 56.25 M delivered at the beginning of the year, which the Northern countries can deliver at the beginning of the year, and the remaining 50 M can be delivered at the end of the year.

INDEX

Aaron, Henry, 8
Absolute advantage, 110
Acid rain, 69
AFL-CIO, 18, 105
African Human Rights, Opportunity, Partnership and Empowerment Act (African HOPE), 101
African Monetary Fund, 90
Aggregate demand, 36-37, 61-62, 63, 65. *See also* Contagion
Agriculture, 19, 108
Anti-imperialist movements, 72-73
Argentina, 63, 72
Asian Development Bank, 30, 89, 90
Asian development model, 7, 46-48
Asian economic crisis (1997), 1-3, 4, 27-32, 41-49; composite stock index, 27; contagion, 72; IMF failure, 60-61; standard explanations, 41-44; unemployment, 27, 28
Asian Monetary Fund, 53, 89
"Asset swindle," 72-81
Austerity, 52, 54, 55
Autarkic solution, 111-113

Baht (Thailand), 1, 27, 60, 63
Bankers Trust, 35, 58, 59, 82
Bankrupted domestic businesses, 73
Banks, 46-48, 81. *See also* Asian Development Bank, Asian Monetary Fund, Central banks
Berry, John, 13
Blair, Tony, 41, 105
Blecker, Robert, 86
Blustein, Paul, 29, 31, 92
Booms, 6-12
Bottom-up organizing, 102-103, 106
Brat, David, 9
Brazil: and contagion, 63, 64, 72; financial crisis, 3, 28, 32, 54, 104; IMF bailouts, 28, 57, 60, 62, 82; Rio Grande do Sul, 94, 95
Brecher, Jeremy, 21, 91, 98
Bretton Woods, 6, 7, 13, 50, 88, 91

Budget deficits, 37
Bush, George, 50, 51
Buying on margin, 34

CA theory. *See* Comparative advantage (CA) theory
Camdessus, Michel, 4, 31, 41, 42, 44, 60; and IMF, 89, 94; and South Korea, 76
Capital, 7, 14-15, 16, 20, 52, 59; social productivity of, 14-15
Capital controls, 87-89, 91, 92, 107
Capital losses, 37
Capital-labor ratio, 18
Capitalism, 3, 7, 11, 36, 81
Carbon emissions, 22, 23
Central banks, 39, 76, 90, 91
Chaebols, 77, 79
Chase Manhattan, 35, 58, 81
Child labor, 98, 99, 101
Child prostitution, 30
Chile, 88
China, 11-12, 61, 88; and contagion, 62, 63, 72; economic crisis, 29, 32; foreign capital in, 26
Chirac, Jacques, 105
Chon, Chol-Hwan, 76
Choo Won Suh, 80
Citibank, 58, 75
Citicorp, 25
Cline, William, 18
Clinton, Bill, 31, 41, 48, 50, 51, 53; and IMF, 57, 89; and South Korea, 58; and trade battles, 98-101, 105
Cobb, John, Jr., 7, 24
Collins, Carole, 94
Commodity prices, 108
Common property resources, 20-21, 106
Communists, 11-12
Comparative advantage (CA) theory, 14, 110, 111
Competition, 83, 111
Complete markets, 83

119

IMF bailouts, 28, 52-53, 57, 60, 62; and multinational corporations, 73-74, 75; World Bank country brief (1999), 29;

Third world economies, 98; economic development of, 41; exports, 108; and the IMF, 52, 85; and international capital, 43; and multinational corporations (MNCs), 72-81; wages in, 18-20. *See also* Emerging markets

Three-way system of pegs, 91

Tobin, James, 7, 24, 87

Tobin tax, 87, 88, 107

Total return swap, 35

Trade, 16-20, 50, 111-118

Trade battle, 98-101

Trade surpluses, 56

Transparency and disclosure, 41, 42-43, 83

Treaties, 24, 25, 108

Trickle downers, 99, 100

Tropical forests, 22

Tutu, Desmond, 92

U2, 92

Undeveloped economies, 63. *See also* Emerging markets

Unemployment, 9, 15, 26, 54, 80; and aggregate demand, 36; and Asian crash, 27, 28; and exports and imports, 40; in Indonesia, 29, 55; low, 9, 66; of productive resources, 71; in South Korea, 29; urban, 19. *See also* Employment; Labor; Workers

Unemployment rates, 10

United Nations, 6

United States, 29; average real wage, 8; composite stock index, 27; and contagion, 63, 72; economic crisis, 32; economic growth, 9; in emerging markets, 45; export sales, 61; free flow of capital, 50; households as

stockholders, 3, 6, 8; income distribution, 8; purchases of foreign stocks, 45; stock market increases, 3, 9, 65, 66; trade deficits, 66

United States Treasury Department, 41, 78

Uruguay, 63

Veneroso, Frank, 89

Viana de Moraes, Jose Luiz, 95

Volcker, Paul, 27, 43, 71, 84

Wachtel, Howard, 91-92

Wade, Robert, 89

Wages, 71; differentials in, 18; raises in, 59; real, 28, 96-97; in third world economies, 18-19

Warburg Dillon Read, 81

Wealth effect, 65.

Wealth-holding, 37-38, 67, 71

Weisbrot, Mark, 66

Williamson, John, 91, 92

Wolfensohn, James, 89

Women, 5

Won (South Korea), 2, 27, 60, 79

Workers, 5, 9, 37, 98. *See also* Labor; Unemployment

World Bank, 1, 2, 6; annual meeting (1998), 27; and capital controls, 88; and the IMF, 55, 89; Malaysia country brief (1999), 29; and Peru, 54; policy failures of, 41; and Russia, 32; Thailand country brief (1999), 29; Web site, 32

Wriston, Walter, 25

Wyatt, Edward, 44

Yeltsin, Boris, 63

Yen (Japan), 2, 45, 91, 105

Yuan (China), 11, 61, 62

ABOUT SOUTH END PRESS

South End Press is a nonprofit, collectively run book publisher with more than 200 titles in print. Since our founding in 1977, we have tried to meet the needs of readers who are exploring, or are already committed to, the politics of radical social change. Our goal is to publish books that encourage critical thinking and constructive action on the key political, cultural, social, economic, and ecological issues shaping life in the United States and in the world. In this way, we hope to give expression to a wide diversity of democratic social movements and to provide an alternative to the products of corporate publishing.

Through the Institute for Social and Cultural Change, South End Press works with other political media projects—Z magazine; Speakout, a speakers' bureau; and Alternative Radio—to expand access to information and critical analysis.

To order books, please send a check or money order to: South End Press, 7 Brookline Street, #1, Cambridge, MA 02139-4146. Please include $3.50 for postage and handling for the first book and 50 cents for each additional book. To order by credit card, call 1-800-533-8478. Write for a free catalog, or visit our Web site, http://www.lbbs.org/sep/sep.htm.

Related Titles

Looking Forward: Participatory Economics for the Twenty-First Century
by Michael Albert and Robin Hahnel $16

Global Village or Global Pillage:
Economic Reconstruction from the Bottom Up (Second Edition)
by Jeremy Brecher and Tim Costello $16
    Companion documentary also available on VHS cassette
    Narrated by Edward Asner, Produced by Andrea Hubbell $25

50 Years Is Enough: The Case Against the World Bank
and the International Monetary Fund
a Project of Global Exchange, edited by Kevin Danaher $16

Global Visions: Beyond the New World Order
edited by Jeremy Brecher, John Brown Childs, and Jill Cutler $16

Biopiracy: The Plunder of Nature and Knowledge
by Vandana Shiva $13

Triumph of the Market: Essays on Economics, Politics and the Media
by Edward S. Herman $16